10 MINUTE GUIDE TO Word Pro 96 Edition for Windows® 3.11

Jennifer Fulton

que®

A Division of Macmillan Publishing
201 West 103rd Street, Indianapolis, Indiana 46290 USA

For my father, Edward Flynn, who has always believed in me—
With love, your "pick of the litter."

International Standard Book Number: 1-56761-310-1
Library of Congress Catalog Card Number: 93-72009

98 97 96 95 8 7 6 5 4 3 2 1

Interpretation of the printing code: the rightmost double-digit number is the year of the book's printing; the rightmost single-digit number is the number of the book's printing. For example, a printing code of 95-1 shows that the first printing of the book was in 1995.

Screen reproductions in this book were created by means of the program Collage Plus from Inner Media, Inc., Hollis, NH.

Printed in the United States of America

Publisher: Roland Elgey
Vice President and Publisher: Marie Butler-Knight
Editorial Services Director: Elizabeth Keaffaber
Publishing Manager: Barry Pruett
Managing Editor: Michael Cunningham
Development Editor: Heather Stith
Technical Editor: C. Herbert Feltner
Production Editor: Phil Kitchel
Copy Editor: Anne Owen
Book Designer: Kim Scott
Indexer: Kathy Venable
Production: Chad Dressler, DiMonique Ford, John Hulse, Clair Schweinler, Michael Thomas

Contents

Introduction

Congratulations! You just bought Word Pro, and now you're anxious to get to work. But because you're already somewhat familiar with your computer, you're not looking forward to having to wade through several manuals before you can write a simple letter.

With your busy schedule, what you really want is a simple, straightforward guide that teaches you what you need to know, without a bunch of extra information that you'll never use.

Does that about sum it up?

Welcome to the *10 Minute Guide to Word Pro 96 Edition for Windows 3.11*

Because most people don't have the luxury of sitting down uninterrupted for hours at a time to learn Word Pro, this *10 Minute Guide* does not attempt to teach you everything about the program. Instead, this book focuses on the most-used features. Each feature is presented in a single, self-contained lesson, designed to take 10 minutes or less to complete. So whenever you have ten minutes, you can complete a lesson on how to edit, save, or even print a document.

In addition, this *10 Minute Guide* teaches you about Word Pro without relying on technical jargon. The easy-to-follow explanations and numbered lists tell you exactly what keys to press and what options to select. With the *10 Minute Guide to Word Pro*, learning to use the program is quick and easy.

Why You Need This Book

The *10 Minute Guide to Word Pro* is for anyone who

- Wants to learn how to get around Word Pro quickly and easily.
- Needs to learn only the steps necessary to accomplish particular goals.
- Wants a clear-cut, plain-English guide that presents the basic features of the program.

How This Book Is Organized

The *10 Minute Guide* consists of a series of lessons ranging from basics (such as starting the program) to a few more advanced features (such as working with tables).

If this is your first encounter with Word Pro, work through Lessons 1 through 9 in order. These lessons lead you through the process of creating, editing, saving, and printing your documents. Subsequent lessons tell you how to use the more advanced features to change line spacing and page margins, set tabs, manage styles, and work with frames and columns.

Icons and Conventions Used in This Book

The following icons have been added throughout the book to help you find your way around:

Timesaver Tip icons offer shortcuts and hints for using the program efficiently.

Plain English icons define new terms.

Panic Button icons appear where new users often run into trouble.

You will find the following conventions that clarify the steps you must perform:

On-screen text Any text that appears on-screen appears in bold.

What you type The information you type appears in bold and color.

Commands and Options The names of menus, commands, buttons, and key combinations that you select appear in color.

Key+Key Combinations In many cases, you must press a two-key key combination in order to enter a command; for example, "Press Ctrl+X." In such cases, hold down the first key and press the second key.

For Further Reference Consult . . .

If you decide after completing this book that you want a more detailed guide to using Word Pro, I suggest the following book from Que:

Special Edition Using Word Pro for Windows by Sue Plumley and Robert Weberg.

Trademarks

Acknowledgments

Thanks to everyone who helped on this book, especially Heather Stith, Phil Kitchel, Anne Owen, and Herb Feltner. I miss you guys!

Lesson 1

Starting Word Pro and Creating a Document

In this lesson, you'll learn how to start Word Pro. You'll also learn how to select the document you want to work on or how to start a new document.

Starting Word Pro

Starting Word Pro is like starting any other Windows program. To start Word Pro, follow these steps:

1. From Program Manager, double-click on the Lotus Applications group icon. The Lotus Applications program group window opens.

2. Double-click on the Lotus Word Pro icon. The Word Pro window opens, and the Welcome to Lotus Word Pro dialog box appears.

When you start Word Pro, you have a choice: you can either start a new document or open an existing document to make changes to it. In the next section, you'll learn how to create a new document. See the last section in this lesson for help in opening an existing document.

Creating a New Document

When creating a new document, you can select a SmartMaster to help you get started, or you can begin with a plain document. Using a SmartMaster helps you easily create professional-looking documents such as business letters, memos, fax cover sheets, reports, and newsletters. That's because after you select the appropriate SmartMaster, you simply click in the indicated areas and add the required information. For example, to complete a letter, you would select a letter SmartMaster, then use the Click Here Blocks to type your addressee's name and address, and to add the body text and signature.

> **SmartMaster** A template you can use to quickly create a professional-looking document. SmartMasters are already formatted for you, and they contain Click Here Blocks to help you complete the document quickly.

Plain English

To create a new document from the Welcome to Lotus Word Pro dialog box, follow these steps:

1. If necessary, click on the Create a New Document from a SmartMaster tab (see Figure 1.1).
2. If you don't want to use a SmartMaster, click on Create a Plain Document. You can then skip the rest of these steps.
3. If you want to use a SmartMaster, select it from the Select a recently used SmartMaster list. Or, if you prefer, click on the More SmartMasters button, select a different SmartMaster, and then click on OK to return

to the Welcome to Lotus Word Pro dialog box. When you select a SmartMaster, it appears in the preview area.

Click on this tab to start a new document.

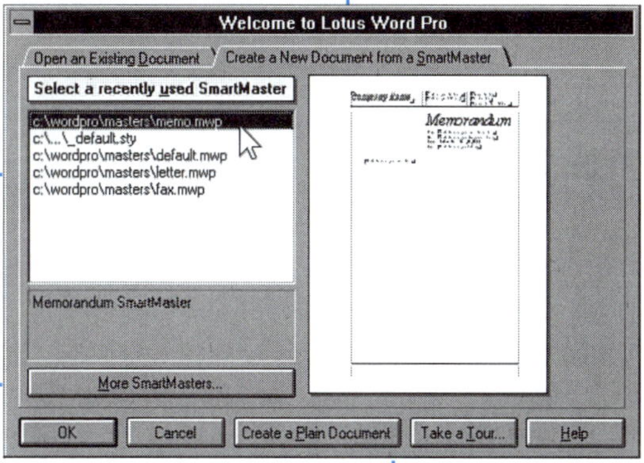

Select a recently used SmartMaster from this list, or search for more SmartMasters.

Click here to create a plain document Preview area.

Figure 1.1 The Welcome to Lotus Word Pro dialog box.

4. Click on OK to close the Welcome to Lotus Word Pro dialog box.

Tour Time If this is your first visit to the world of Word Pro, you might want to take a short tour to get more familiar. Just click on the Take a Tour button in the Welcome to Lotus Word Pro dialog box.

If you select a plain document, Word Pro opens an empty document for you to start typing in. See Lesson 4 for help. If you selected a SmartMaster, see the upcoming section for help.

Using a SmartMaster

SmartMasters contain predefined styles and Click Here Blocks. You can use styles to quickly format specific sections of the document, such as a heading or an opening paragraph. The Click Here Blocks guide you through completing the document. To use a Click Here Block, just click on it and then type your text, as shown in Figure 1.2. What you type replaces the Click Here Block. In some cases, when you click on the block, a dialog box appears to help you select a picture (or whatever) from a list. Just make your selection and click on OK to close the dialog box.

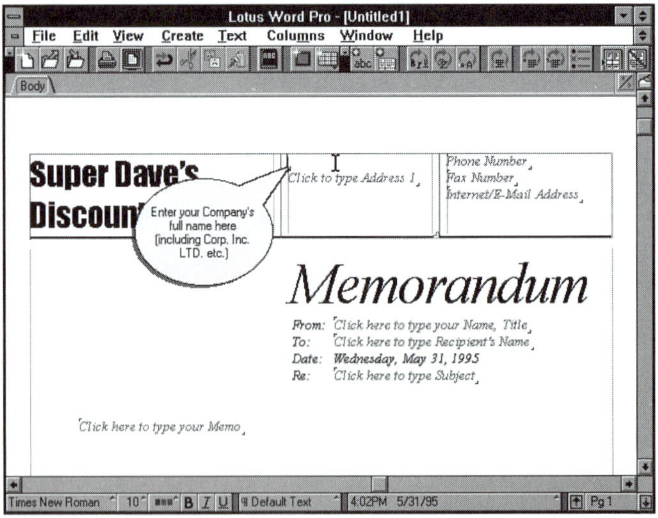

Figure 1.2 Just click and type to complete your SmartMaster document.

Style A set of properties that define how something looks. For example, you might create a Heading style with big, bold text and use it to format all of the headings in a report so that they look alike.

Plain English

Creating a New Document Later in the Work Session

When you start Word Pro, it's easy to create a new document. But suppose you've been working on a document and now you want to start a new one.

All you have to do is open the File menu and select the New command, or click on the File New SmartIcon. (If you're not sure what a SmartIcon is, jump to Lesson 2.) You'll see a dialog box similar to the one you saw when you started Word Pro, with a few minor changes. The steps for creating a new document with this dialog box are similar to those listed earlier: just click on the appropriate tab to select the SmartMaster you want, and then click on OK to create the new document.

Opening an Existing Document

To work on a previously saved document, you have to open it. To open an existing document, do the following:

1. In the Welcome to Lotus Word Pro dialog box, click on the Open an Existing Document tab (see Figure 1.3).
2. Select a recently used document from those listed, or click on the Browse for More Files… button to open a different document.

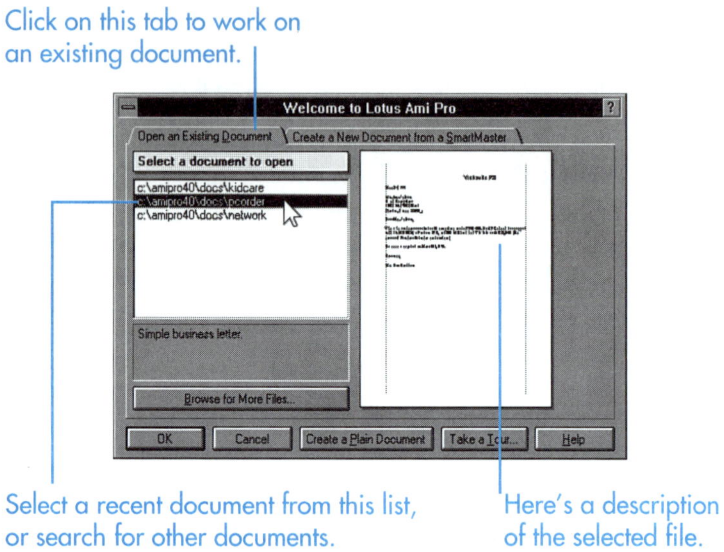

Figure 1.3 Opening an existing document.

Get a Clear Description If you're having difficulty finding the exact document you want, look in the description area. If you entered a description when you created the selected document, the description will be displayed here. To enter a description for an open document, open the File menu, select Document Properties, and then select the Document command. In the Document dialog box that appears, enter the description you want in the Description text box.

3. If you click on the Browse for New Files... button, you'll see the Open dialog box, shown in Figure 1.4. Change to the drive and directory of the document you want to open and then select it from the File name list box.

Open Sesame You can open several documents at once by pressing Ctrl and selecting each document from the list.

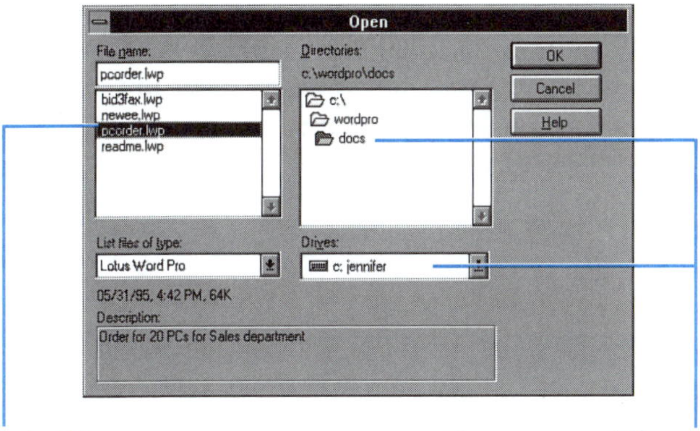

Figure 1.4 The Open dialog box.

4. Click on OK to open the document.

Opening an Existing Document Later in the Work Session

Once you start Word Pro and work for a while, you can open additional documents. Just open the File menu and select the Open command, or click on the File Open SmartIcon. (For help on SmartIcons, see Lesson 2.) You'll see the Open dialog box shown in Figure 1.4, so just follow steps 3 and 4 in the preceding section.

Fast Open You can quickly open a document you recently worked on by opening the File menu and selecting the document from those listed at the bottom of the menu.

By the way, you can have many documents open at the same time and switch between them as often as you like; you don't have to close (or put away) an existing document to open a new one. If you want more details, see Lesson 11.

In this lesson, you learned how to start Word Pro. You also learned how to create a new document or open an existing document. In the next lesson, you'll take a quick tour of the Word Pro window and learn how to exit (quit) Word Pro.

Lesson 2

Touring and Then Quitting Word Pro

In this lesson, you'll learn the parts of a basic Word Pro window and how to exit Word Pro.

Understanding the Parts of a Word Pro Window

Whether you're working on a new or existing document, you'll enter your text, tables, charts, and so on, within the Word Pro window. The typical Word Pro window shown in Figure 2.1 has many parts.

SmartIcons A palette of buttons you can click on instead of selecting a command. For example, you could select the File Save icon instead of the File, Save command to save the current document. You'll learn more about using SmartIcons in the next section.

Division Tabs These tabs allow you to divide a long document into logical sections, making it easier to work. You'll find out more about Division tabs in Lesson 19.

Status Bar This displays the current style, font, and point size of the selected text, the status of the Caps Lock and Num Lock keys, and more. You'll learn more about the Status bar in the next section.

Text Area The area of the Word Pro window where your text is displayed.

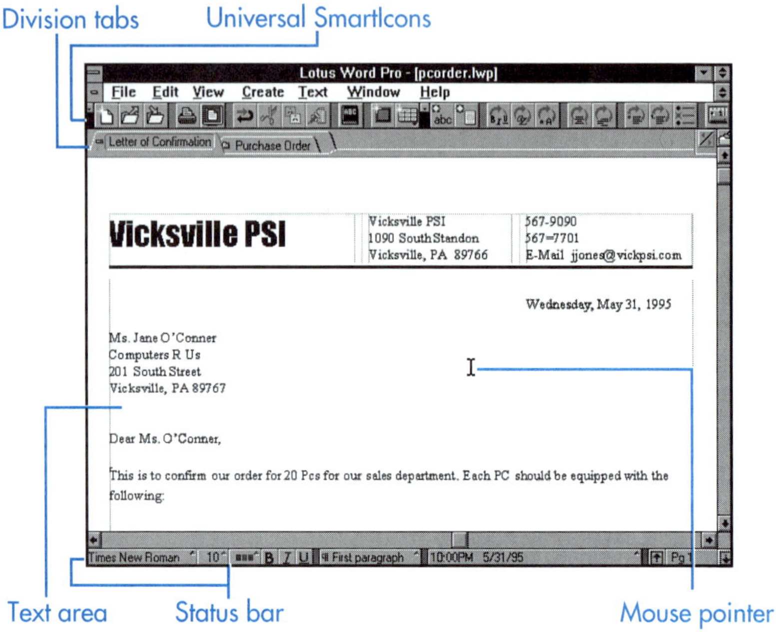

Figure 2.1 A typical Word Pro window.

Using SmartIcons

SmartIcons allow you to quickly perform common tasks at the click of a button. To use a SmartIcon, simply click on it. For example, to open an existing document, simply click on the File Open SmartIcon.

When you first start Word Pro, it displays the Universal Iconbar, as shown in Figure 2.1. A second set of SmartIcons is also usually displayed, but this set varies based on what you are currently working on. For example, if you're in the Text area, you'll see the Text Iconbar. If you move to the Header area at the top of most documents, you'll see the Header Iconbar. Because what's displayed varies based on what you're currently working on, Word Pro is said to be *context-sensitive*. This context-sensitivity affects other things, as you'll see later on in this lesson.

To discover what a particular SmartIcon does, simply move your mouse pointer over the icon. A small help "bubble" appears with a description of the icon (see Figure 2.2).

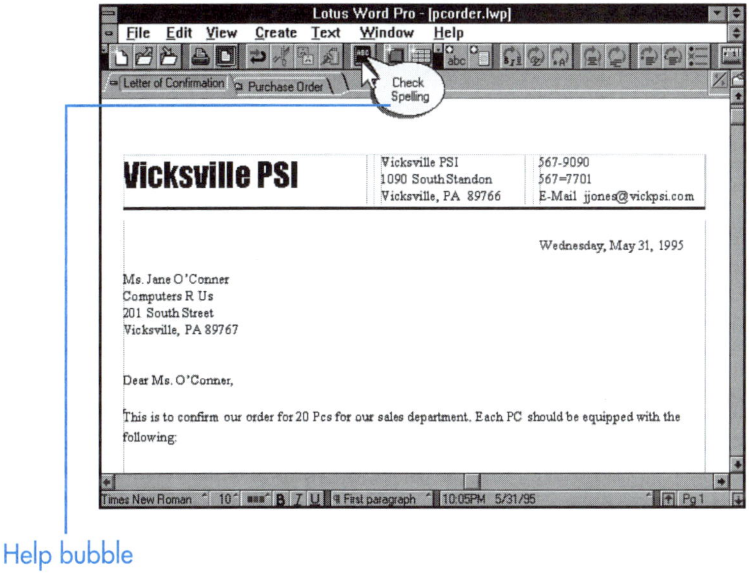

Figure 2.2 The help bubble tells you what action a particular SmartIcon performs.

You can drag a SmartIcon into the text area to make it more convenient to use; simply press Ctrl and click on the SmartIcon. Drag the SmartIcon into the text area and release the mouse button. You can hide a set of SmartIcons and/or force a particular set to display. You can also customize the Universal Iconbar (or any other SmartIcon set) with the icons you use the most. You'll learn how to do this and more in Lesson 20.

Using the Status Bar

The Status bar shown in Figure 2.3 provides important information, such as the current date and time. It also allows you to quickly change how text looks, in addition to providing an easy way to move from page to page within your document. You'll find out more about each of these functions in upcoming lessons.

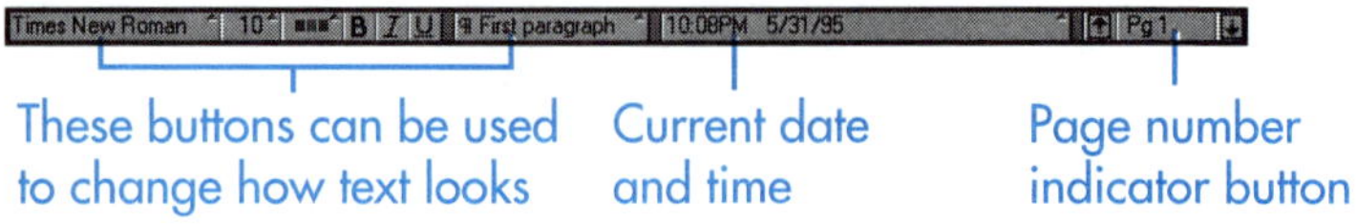

Figure 2.3 The Status bar.

To use a button on the Status bar, simply click on it. For example, to jump to a particular page, click on the Page Number Indicator button on the Status bar to open the Go To dialog box.

Using Cycle Keys

You can use a cycle key (or the corresponding SmartIcon) to quickly "cycle" through a list of similar changes. To use a cycle key (or cycle SmartIcon), select the text you want to change, then press (or click) repeatedly until you get the effect you want. (You'll learn how to select text in Lesson 5.)

Table 2.1 lists the types of changes you can make with a cycle key.

Table 2.1 Word Pro's Cycle Keys

Key	Function
F2	Changes the style of selected paragraphs
F3	Changes the font of selected text
F4	Changes the point size of selected text
F5	Changes the attributes (such as bold, italic, and so on) of selected text

Key	Function
F6	Changes the alignment of selected paragraphs
F7	Changes the indentation of selected paragraphs
F8	Cycles through various bulleted list styles
F9	Cycles through various numbered list styles
F11	Selects as many sentences as you like, beginning with the current sentence
F12	Selects as many paragraphs as you like, beginning with the current paragraph

You'll learn more about making these changes in upcoming lessons. After that, if you want to adjust the types of changes associated with a particular cycle key, just open the File menu and select User Setup. Select CycleKey Setup and then choose the cycle key whose function you want to change. Make your selections for each cycle and then click on OK.

Activating a Pop-Up Menu

As you work on your document, you may often find it convenient to use *pop-up menus*. A pop-up menu appears within the text area near where you're working, and you can use it to quickly select a command appropriate to the current situation. For example, if you select a paragraph and then activate a pop-up menu, the commands appropriate to working with paragraphs will appear. To activate a pop-up menu, press the right mouse button.

Introducing the InfoBox

There are many ways to change your document. For example, you may want to change the size, alignment, and color of some text. The Text InfoBox, shown in Figure 2.4, is a special dialog box from which you can make all of these changes and more in one step. Just click on the various tabs to move from section to section. You'll learn the purpose of each tab in upcoming lessons.

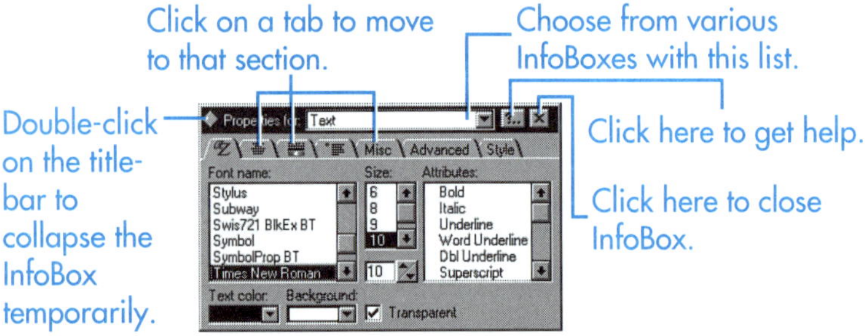

Figure 2.4 The Text InfoBox.

You might encounter other InfoBoxes, such as the Frame InfoBox or the Page Layout InfoBox, to name two. To display an InfoBox for a particular object in your document, select the object, right-click, and then choose the Properties command from the pop-up menu. As you make your changes with the InfoBox, they appear within the document so you can see how they look. To close an InfoBox, click once on its close button, or double-click on its Control-menu icon.

You can scroll up an InfoBox like a window shade, to place it temporarily out of the way. Just double-click on the title bar of the InfoBox. Double-click again to redisplay the InfoBox.

If you need help with a particular pane of an InfoBox, click on the Help button (the button with the question mark on it).

Quitting Word Pro

To quit (exit) Word Pro and return to Windows, follow these steps:

1. Open the File menu.
2. Click on Exit Word Pro.

If you have unsaved documents open, Word Pro prompts you to save them. You'll learn more about saving documents in Lesson 7. After you save your documents, Word Pro closes itself and returns you to Windows.

Fast Close You can also double-click on the control-menu icon (the large minus sign) in the upper left-hand corner of the Word Pro window to exit.

In this lesson, you took a quick tour of the more common elements of the Word Pro screen. In addition, you learned how to exit Word Pro. In the next lesson, you'll learn the special aspects of the Word Pro Help system.

Lesson

Getting Help

In this lesson, you'll learn how the Word Pro Help system differs from the Help systems found in other Windows programs.

Using Ask the Expert

One nice feature of the Word Pro Help system that's not often found in other programs is Ask the Expert. With it, you ask Word Pro *in your own words* how to perform a particular task, and Ask the Expert displays the appropriate steps within the Help system to guide you.

For example, you could ask, "How do I number pages in my document?" Ask the Expert would then display the steps shown in Figure 3.1.

To use Ask the Expert, follow these steps:

1. If necessary, display the Expert bar by opening the Help menu and by selecting Ask the Expert.
2. Type your question in the "How do I..." box (see Figure 3.1).
3. Click on the OK button. A Help window is displayed.
4. If necessary, you can select another task from the list box and click on OK to view that topic instead.
5. When you're through, close any open Help windows and then click on the Done button to close the Expert bar.

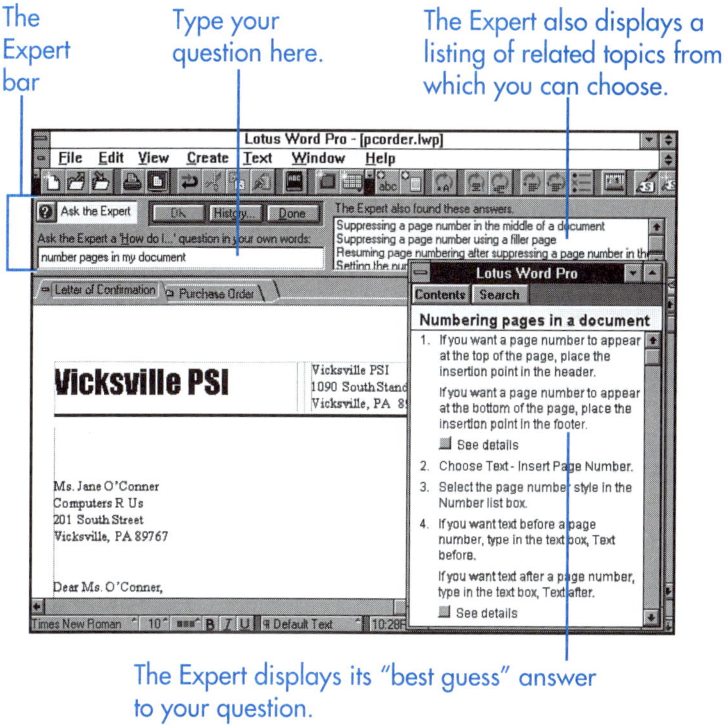

Figure 3.1 Ask the Expert displays the steps to perform your task.

Fast Answers Leave the Expert bar displayed all the time (by not clicking on the Done button) for quicker access to the Help system. By the way, you can close Help windows without removing the Expert bar from the screen by simply double-clicking on their control-menu boxes.

You can display a list of previously asked questions by clicking on the History button. Select a question from the list and then click on OK to place the question in the "How do I..." box. Click on OK again to view a Help window with the answer.

Using Bubble Help

Bubble Help is displayed when the mouse pointer is placed over a SmartIcon, as shown in Figure 3.2. Bubble Help provides an easy way for you to identify the purpose of a particular SmartIcon.

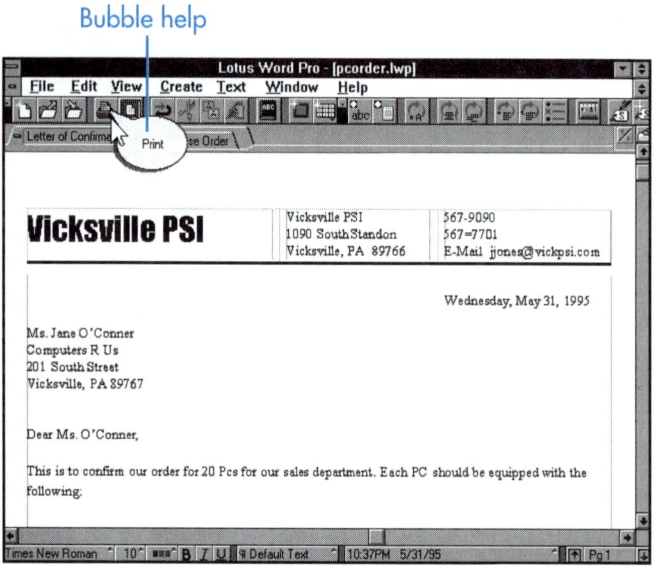

Figure 3.2 Bubble Help identifies SmartIcons for you.

By default, Bubble Help is turned on. However, you can turn it off if you want to by following these steps:

1. Open the File menu and select User Setup.
2. Select SmartIcons Setup.
3. Deselect the Show SmartIcon descriptions (bubble help) box.
4. Click on OK.

Using Demos and Assistants

Throughout the Help system, you'll encounter various *demos* and *Assistants* that can guide you through the steps necessary to complete a difficult task. The demos show you what to do, then ask you to complete the step yourself. An Assistant is a special dialog box with tabs for each step in a complex process. With the tabs, you can easily move back and forth through the steps, changing your selections when needed.

To use a demo, follow these steps:

1. From within a help window, click on the Demo button (see Figure 3.3).

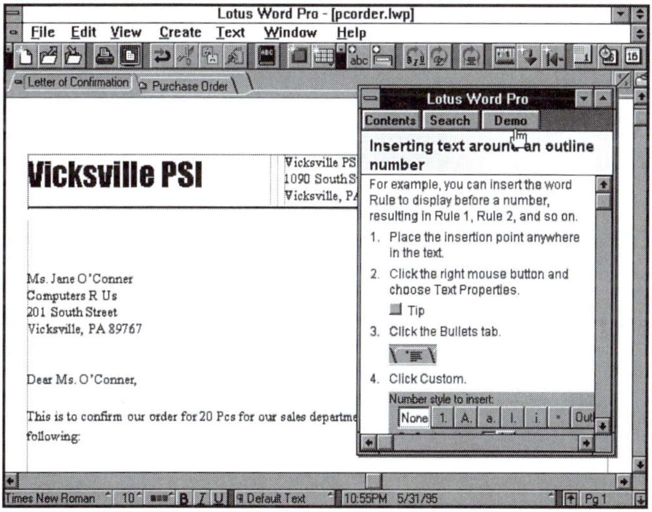

Figure 3.3 Watch as a demo steps you through a task.

2. Watch as the demo completes the first step, then complete that step yourself by performing the same actions. Repeat the process for additional steps.

3. When the demo is over, close the Help window.

Assistants appear when you select a complex task, such as Mail Merge, TOC, Index, or TeamReview. The Assistant for the Mail Merge command is shown in Figure 3.4.

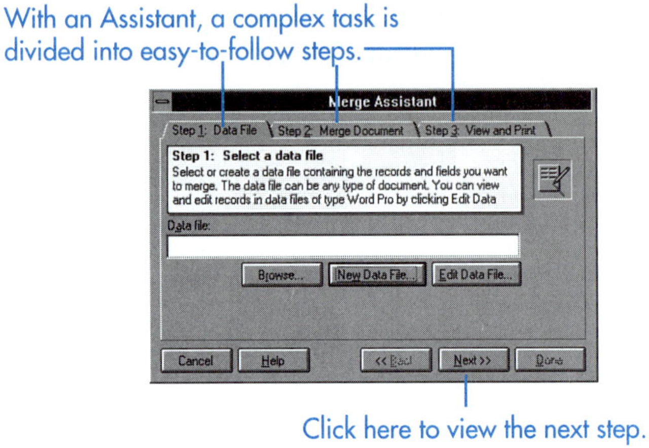

Figure 3.4 Assistants step you through complex tasks.

To use an Assistant, do the following:

1. Make your selections for the first step.
2. Click on the Next >> button.
3. Make your selections for the next step, and then click on Next >>. You can change the selections for a previous step by clicking on Back >>.
4. After making your selections for the last step, click on Done.

In this lesson, you learned about the special features of the Word Pro Help system. In the next lesson, you'll learn how to enter text into a document.

Lesson 4

Adding Text

In this lesson, you'll learn how to enter text in a Word Pro document.

Entering Text

When you start a new document, Word Pro automatically places your cursor at the top of the document window so that you are ready to start entering text. To enter text, simply start typing. As you type, your words appear on the screen, like words from a typewriter.

Unlike using a typewriter, *you should not press Enter at the end of every line.* If you press Enter at the end of every line, Word Pro treats each of those lines as a separate paragraph. Instead, just let Word Pro automatically advance the text to the next line at the appropriate point. This feature is called *word wrapping.*

Word Wrap In word wrapping, words are automatically advanced to the next line of a paragraph when they bump into the right margin.

With word wrapping, you can insert words into the middle of a paragraph, and the rest of the paragraph is automatically adjusted downward. If you change the right margin, paragraphs adjust automatically to fit between the new margins.

Press the Enter key only at the end of a paragraph. You should also press Enter at the end of any section of text that should be treated separately from the next section (such as a title).

Press Tab to indent a paragraph (or use the Indent feature, as explained in Lesson 16). *Don't press the Spacebar* because, depending on the size of the characters you use, your paragraphs might not align properly. So use the Tab key instead.

Also, you should not use the Spacebar to move around a document; instead, use the techniques discussed in the section "Moving Around a Document."

Correcting Small Mistakes

As you type, the blinking cursor (or *insertion point*) follows you. What you type is always placed at this insertion point. If you want to correct something you already typed, you can move this insertion point backward in the document. See the section, "Moving Around the Document" for help.

> **Insertion Point** The place where the cursor is located within the text. What you type is placed to the right of the insertion point.
>
> Plain English

When you type text into a document, it is assumed that you want to insert text and not type over existing characters. To type over existing text, you must turn on *overtype mode* by pressing the Insert key. Press the Insert key again to switch back to Insert mode.

Overtype Mode The opposite of Insertion mode. When you're in Overtype mode, the characters you type replace existing characters in the document.

Correcting typing mistakes in Word Pro is easy. Simply press the Backspace key to back up and erase text, or move the cursor (insertion point) to a character you want to remove and press Delete. (See the next section for help in moving the cursor.) You can delete a large section of text by selecting it first; see Lesson 5 for help.

Saved by Undo You can undo your last change by opening the Edit menu and selecting Undo or by clicking on the Undo SmartIcon. See Lesson 5 for more help.

Moving Around a Document

To move the insertion point with the mouse, simply click anywhere within the document. If you can't see the point to which you want to move, use the scroll bars to scroll through the document, then click inside the document at the appropriate point. You can drag the scroll box up or down the vertical scroll bar to jump quickly to another page within the document. When you drag the scroll box, a page gauge appears, to help you calculate approximately where to drag the scroll box to jump to a particular page (see Figure 4.1).

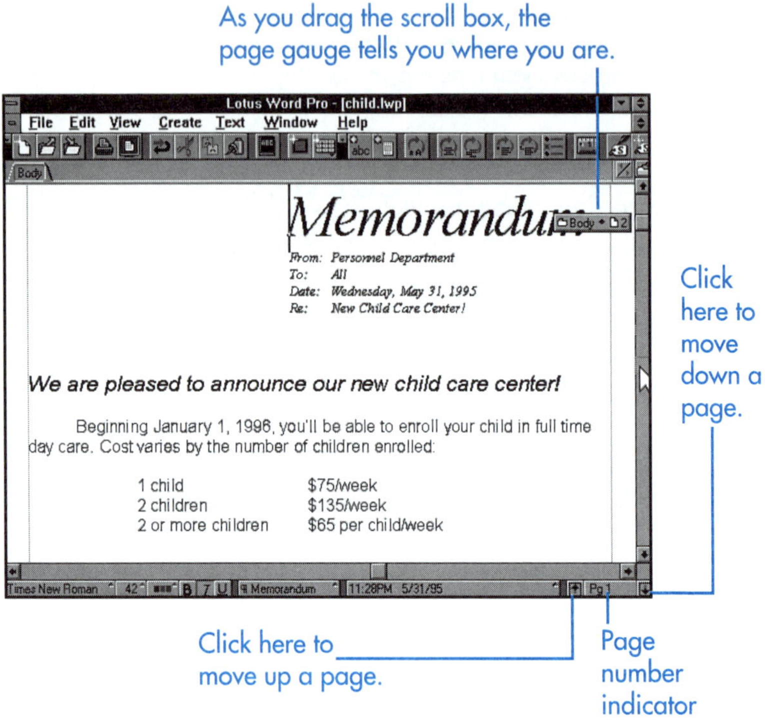

Figure 4.1 Scrolling reveals the page gauge.

You can move forward or backward one page by clicking the Page Up or Page Down indicators on the Status bar. You can also jump to a particular page with Go To:

1. Click on the page number indicator on the Status bar. The Go To dialog box shown in Figure 4.2 appears.

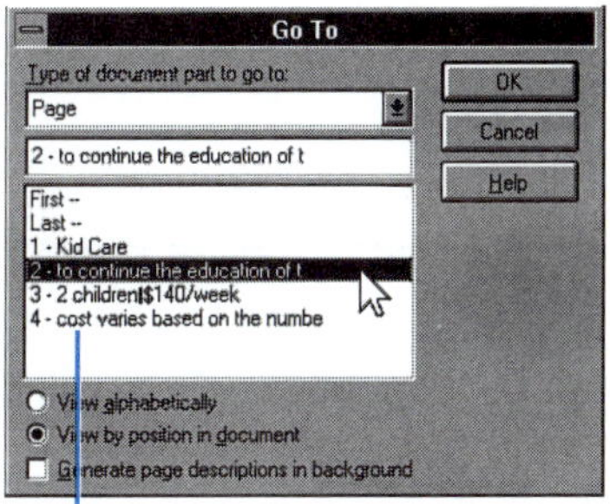

Figure 4.2 Use Go To to move to a particular page in the document.

2. If necessary, select Page from the Type of document part to go to list.
3. Select the page you want to go to from the list. To help you find the page, the first few words on each page are displayed after the page number.
4. Click on OK.

If your document is divided into tabbed parts, you can click on a tab at the top of the window to move directly to that section. See Lesson 19 for help on creating sections and divisions.

Table 4.1 lists the ways you can move the insertion point with the keyboard.

Table 4.1 Moving through a Document with the Keyboard

To Move...	Press This...
Up or down one line	↑ or ↓
Left or right one character	← or →
One word left or right	Ctrl+← or Ctrl+→
To the next sentence	Ctrl+. (period)
To the previous sentence	Ctrl+, (comma)
Up or down one paragraph	Ctrl+↑ or Ctrl+↓
Up or down one screen	Page Up or Page Down
Up one page	Ctrl+Page Up
Down one page	Ctrl+Page Down
Beginning of the line	Home
End of the line	End
Beginning of the document	Ctrl+Home
End of the document	Ctrl+End

Adding the Date and Time to a Document

To insert the date or time into a document, follow these steps:

1. Open the Text menu and select Insert Other.
2. Select Date/Time. The Insert Date/Time dialog box shown in Figure 4.3 appears.

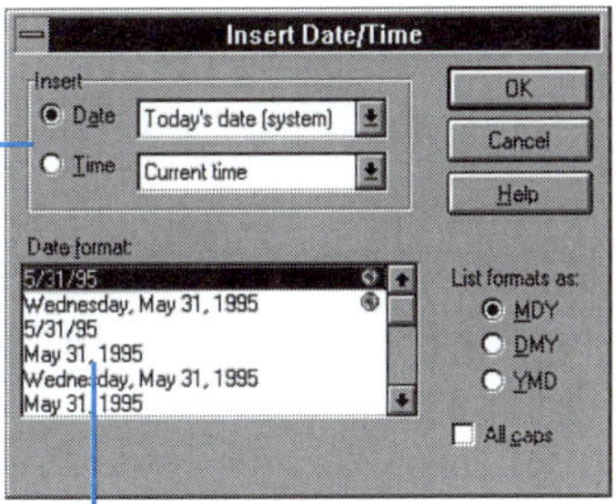

Figure 4.3 The Insert Date/Time dialog box.

3. Select either the Date or Time option button. (You cannot insert both the date and the time at once; you must repeat these steps to add them both.)

4. Select an option from the corresponding (Date or Time) drop-down list box.

System vs. Static If you insert today's date as a system date, that date will change every time you open the document. This keeps the date you inserted current. If you want to insert today's date and not have it update every time you use the document, choose Static.

5. Select the Date or Time format. Choose other options as needed.

6. Click on OK. The date (or the time) is inserted at the cursor.

Adding a Page Break

Normally, all you have to do is type, and a new page appears when needed. But if you want a new page to appear *before* you fill the current page, you must insert a page break. For example, if you just typed a cover page for a report, you can insert a page break and start the body of the report on a new page.

Word Pro inserts soft page breaks automatically. These soft page breaks move as needed when you add or delete text from a page. When you insert a manual page break, it is considered a "hard" page break, because it does not move. So if you insert a page break after a particular paragraph, that page break stays there until you delete it.

To insert a page break, follow these steps:

1. If necessary, press Enter to move to a blank line.
2. Open the Text menu.
3. Select Insert Page Break. A page break marker (a page icon followed by the words "Page Break") is inserted at the cursor, and you're presented with a new page.

Fast Break You can also press Ctrl+Enter to insert a page break.

To delete a page break, click on the page break marker and press Backspace.

In this lesson, you learn how to add text and edit mistakes. You also learned how to insert the date, time, or a page break. In the next lesson, you'll learn how to copy, move, and delete text.

Lesson 5

Editing Text

In this lesson, you'll learn how to copy, move, and delete text in a Word Pro document. You'll also learn how to undo changes you make, and find and replace text.

Selecting Text

There are many changes you might make when editing a document. For example, you might move a sentence from the beginning of a paragraph to the end. In any case, to move, copy, or delete text, you select it first and then perform the desired command.

To select text with the mouse, follow these steps:

1. Place the mouse pointer over the first letter in the text to be selected and click.
2. Drag the mouse until you reach the end of the text you want to select.
3. Release the mouse button, and the text you select is highlighted in reverse video. Figure 5.1 shows the words **Dear Ms. O'Conner** being selected.

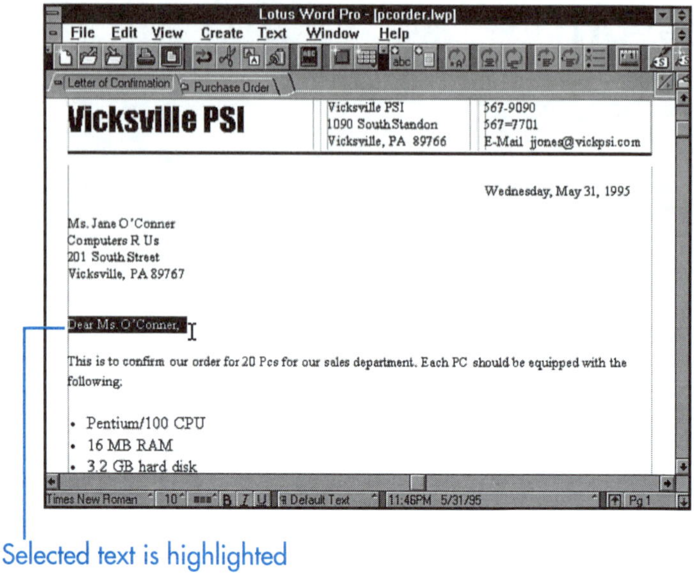

Figure 5.1. The text you select is displayed in reverse video.

Did You Select the Wrong Text? To "unselect" the text that you have just selected, either select some other text or click anywhere in the document. You can also press one of the arrow keys to unselect text.

You can select multiple words, sentences, or paragraphs by performing the action listed in the table and then *dragging* the mouse. For example, to select multiple sentences, press Ctrl, click on the first sentence, and then drag to select additional sentences.

Table 5.1 shows some shortcuts you can use when selecting text with the mouse.

Table 5.1 Mouse Text Selection Shortcuts

Text to Select	Action
Word	Double-click on the word.
Sentence	Press the Ctrl key and click on the sentence.
Paragraph	Press the Ctrl key and double-click on the paragraph.

Fast Selection You can select text quickly by clicking in the text and selecting the appropriate command from the Text menu. Just open the Text menu and choose Select. Then choose either Word, Sentence, Paragraph, or Entire Division.

To select text with the keyboard, follow these steps:

1. Place the cursor over the first letter in the text to be selected and press the Shift key.
2. With the Shift key depressed, use the right arrow key to highlight the text you want to select.

In addition, you can use the following cycle keys to quickly select text. (If you want to know more about cycle keys, see Lesson 2.)

Key	Function
F11	Selects as many sentences as you like, beginning with the current sentence
F12	Selects as many paragraphs as you like, beginning with the current paragraph

Quick Keyboard Select You can combine the keys you use to move around a document with the Shift key to select larger amounts of text. For example, if you press Home, you move to the end of the current line. If you press Shift+Home, you'll select all the text from the cursor to the end of the line. See Lesson 4 for a list of keys to use in moving through a document.

Deleting and Replacing Text

You can delete a small mistake as you type by simply pressing Backspace. But to delete a larger section of text, follow these steps:

1. Select the text you want to delete.
2. Press the Delete key.

Instead of just deleting the text, you can delete it and replace it with new text in one step. Just select the text you want to replace, and then type the new text. What you type replaces the selected text.

Copying and Moving Text

Copying and moving text is often the key to "fine-tuning" a document. Because of this, the techniques you'll learn in this section will probably be the ones you'll use the most. The most common way to copy or move text involves a method called *drag and drop*. Follow these steps to drag and drop text:

1. Select the text you want to copy or move.
2. Position the mouse pointer over the selection so that a hand appears.
3. To copy the text, press and hold the Ctrl key. To move text, skip this step.

4. Drag the text to where you want it to be copied or moved.

5. Release the mouse button to "drop" the text.

If you want to copy or move text to a place that is not visible within the document, the simplest method is to use the Windows Clipboard. Follow these steps:

> **Clipboard** The Windows Clipboard is a tiny area of your computer's memory where data is stored temporarily as you move or copy it from one place to another. Data placed on the Clipboard can then be copied or moved from within the same document, from one document to another, and also from one Windows program to another (provided both of the separate programs support the use of the Clipboard).

1. Select the text that you want to copy or move.

2. Open the Edit menu.

3. Select Copy (to copy text) or Cut (to move text). The text is copied or moved to the Clipboard.

4. Click in the document at the point where you want to copy or move the text.

5. Open the Edit menu again.

6. Select Paste, and the text is pasted from the Clipboard and placed at the insertion point.

Notice that whether you copy or move text, the selection is later *pasted* from the Clipboard to the place you indicate. This means that the selection is still on the Clipboard, and so it can be pasted again and again to other locations in the document if you want. Note, however, that text remains on the Clipboard only *until it is replaced by some other selection* that you place on the Clipboard with the Copy or Cut commands. Also, the contents of the Clipboard are cleared when you exit Word Pro.

> **Be Careful When You Move Text** When you use the Cut command, the selected text is removed from the document and placed on the Clipboard. If something else is copied to the Clipboard before you finish moving the text, the text that you selected to be moved will be lost.

When you use the Clipboard to copy or move text, there are some shortcuts you can use to avoid using the Edit menu:

- To copy text, select it and press Ctrl+C, or click on the Copy SmartIcon.
- To move (or cut) text, select it and press Ctrl+X, or click on the Cut SmartIcon.
- To paste text, press Ctrl+V, or click on the Paste SmartIcon.

Undoing Your Changes

If you make a change you don't like, such as deleting some text or moving text to the wrong spot, you can undo it. That is, you can undo it *if it represents the last change you made to the document.*

To undo your last change:

- Click on the Undo SmartIcon

  or

- Open the Edit menu and select Undo.

By default, Word Pro saves the last 100 changes you've made to a document. Here's how to undo a change *other than the most recent one*:

1. Open the Edit menu and select Undo/Redo Special. The Undo/Redo dialog box shown in Figure 5.2 appears.

You can select a change to redo if you want.

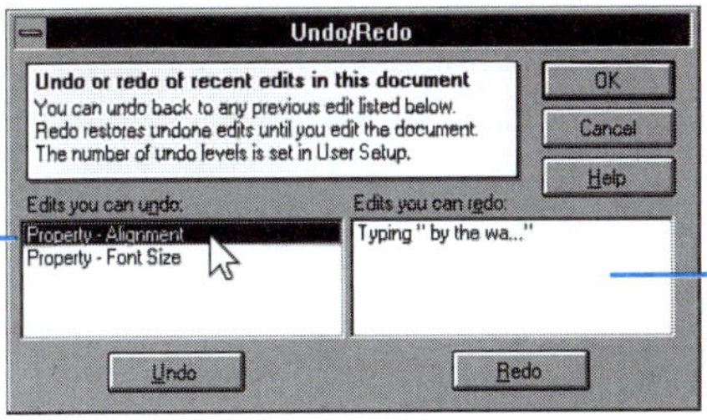

Select a change to undo.

Figure 5.2 The Undo/Redo dialog box lets you undo several levels of changes.

2. Select the edit change you want to undo from the Edits you can undo list Undo list. Selecting anything other than the first change in the list causes earlier changes to also be selected.

3. Click on Undo.

4. If you want to, you can redo a change you've undone by selecting it from the Edits you can redo list Redo list and by clicking on Redo.

5. When you're through, click on OK to return to your document.

Finding and Replacing Text

You can use Word Pro's Find and Replace feature to replace the occurrence of one word or phrase with another. For example, you could replace the name "Ami Pro" with "Word Pro" throughout a document.

You can also use the Find and Replace feature to find text without replacing it. This is helpful when searching for a particular place within a large document.

To find and replace text, follow these steps:

1. Open the Edit menu and select Find & Replace. The Find & Replace review bar appears at the top of the document window, as shown in Figure 5.3.

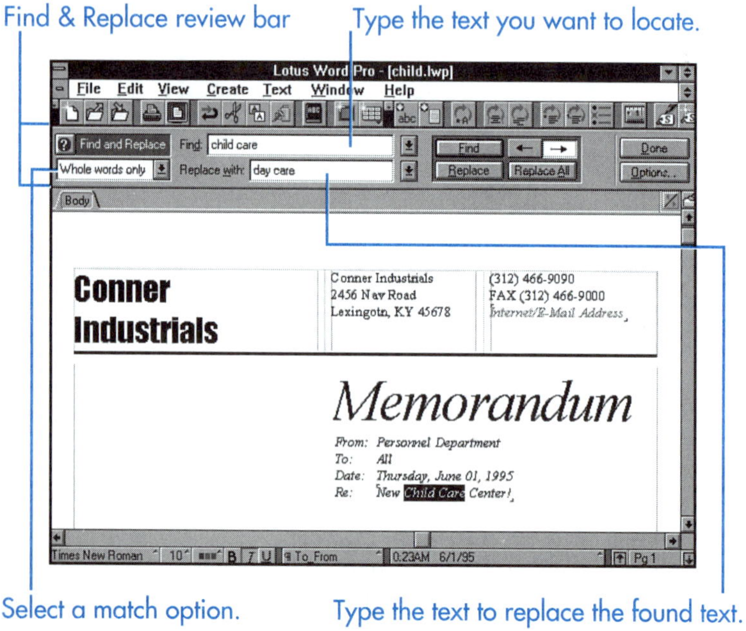

Figure 5.3 Use the Find & Replace review bar to find and replace text.

2. Type the text you want to locate in the Find list box.
3. If you want to replace text (and not just search for it), type the replacement text in the Replace with list box.

Deja Vu? Find & Replace remembers the last four text strings you searched for and replaced, so you may be able to open the list box and select your text if you've searched for it before. Doing so will save you the trouble of typing the text again.

4. If you want to, change the selection in the Match list box. For example, you might want to search for the text *within* a word instead of as a whole word.

5. To change the direction of the search, click on the right or left arrow.

6. Click on Find. Word Pro searches the document in the indicated direction for the text.

Hey, It Didn't Find It! If Word Pro doesn't find your text, it will ask you if you wish to continue. Click on Yes to return to the Find & Replace review bar to search for different text, or click on No to close the Find & Replace review bar.

7. To replace this occurrence only, click on Replace. To replace all occurrences of the found text, click on Replace All.

8. Repeat steps 6 and 7 to continue to search and replace your text.

9. Click on Done to remove the Find & Replace review bar.

More Options You can click on the **Options** button to fine-tune your search. For example, you can replace all occurrences of the italicized word *terrific buy* with a bold, underlined version: **terrific buy**. You can also use *wild cards* to find several similar items. For example, you could use the Options dialog box to search for "Item 75-^?" and locate items 75-1, 75-2, and so on.

In this lesson, you learned various ways to edit text, such as inserting, deleting, copying, and moving. You also learned how to undo your changes, as well as how to find and replace text. In the next lesson, you'll learn how to change the look of text.

Lesson 6

Formatting Text

In this lesson, you'll learn how to place different kinds of emphasis on your words through text formatting.

Changing Text Attributes with the InfoBox

The type of font you select can often affect the way the words you write are interpreted. Fonts can be used to convey a mood, a feeling, or to draw the eye to particular words. In addition, text attributes such as bold, underline, italics, and even the text's size (point size) can lend emphasis and draw the reader to certain text.

> **Font?** Font refers to the combination of typeface (the style of the characters), weight (regular vs. bold), and size. The size of a particular character is measured in points. (One point is equal to 1/72 of an inch.)

You can change the way text looks by changing its *style*, or by changing it manually. The style of text defines all of its attributes, such as the size of the text and whether that text is bold, italic, and so on. Once you create and define a style, you can quickly apply that style to text blocks in order to make the text blocks all look the same. You'll learn more about styles in Lesson 15.

If you don't change the text's style, you can change the way text looks by changing selected attributes with the Text InfoBox. Here's how:

1. Select the text whose attributes you want to change. If you just want to change one word, you don't need to actually select it; instead, just click anywhere inside the word.

2. Open the Text menu and select Text Properties. You can also right-click and select Text Properties from the pop-up menu. The Text InfoBox appears, as shown in Figure 6.1.

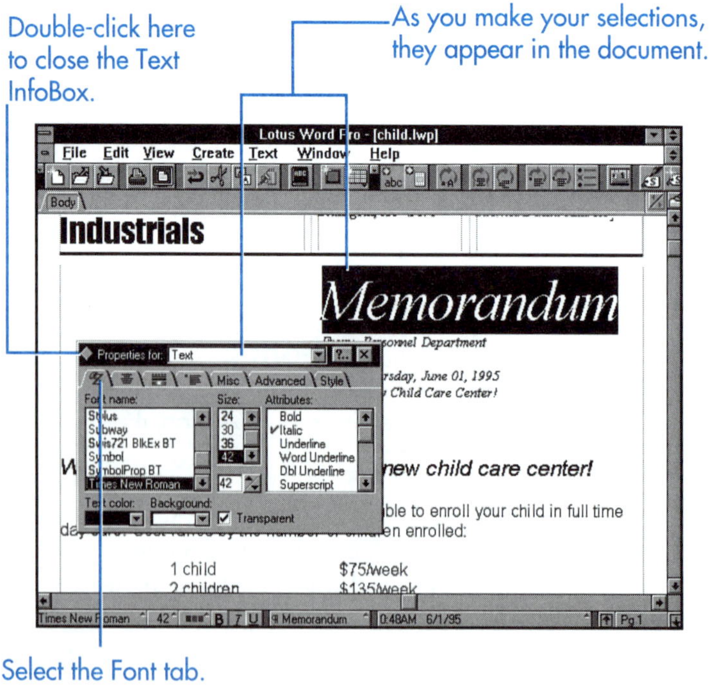

Figure 6.1 The Text InfoBox provides easy access to a text's attributes.

3. If necessary, click on the Font tab.

4. Make the desired changes. For example, to change the font, make a selection from the Font name list box. You can also change the text's size, color, and other attributes.

5. As you make your selections, the change takes place within the document, so you can immediately see how your selections will affect the text. When you're through, you can close the Text InfoBox by double-clicking on the control-menu icon.

Wrong Change! If you make changes to text that you don't like, you can undo *your last change* by clicking on the Undo SmartIcon. In addition, you can remove all formatting from text by opening the Text menu and selecting Normal. However, formatting that comes from the text's style will not be removed. (See Lesson 15 for help on understanding styles.)

Using Other Methods to Change Text Attributes

There are easier ways to change a single attribute than using the Text InfoBox. For example, to change just the font, you can use the Status bar or a cycle key instead of opening the Text InfoBox.

To use the Status bar to change text, follow these steps:

1. Select the text whose attributes you want to change. If you just want to change one word, click anywhere inside the word.

2. Click on the appropriate button on the Status bar. For example, to change the font size, click on the Font Size button (see Figure 6.2).

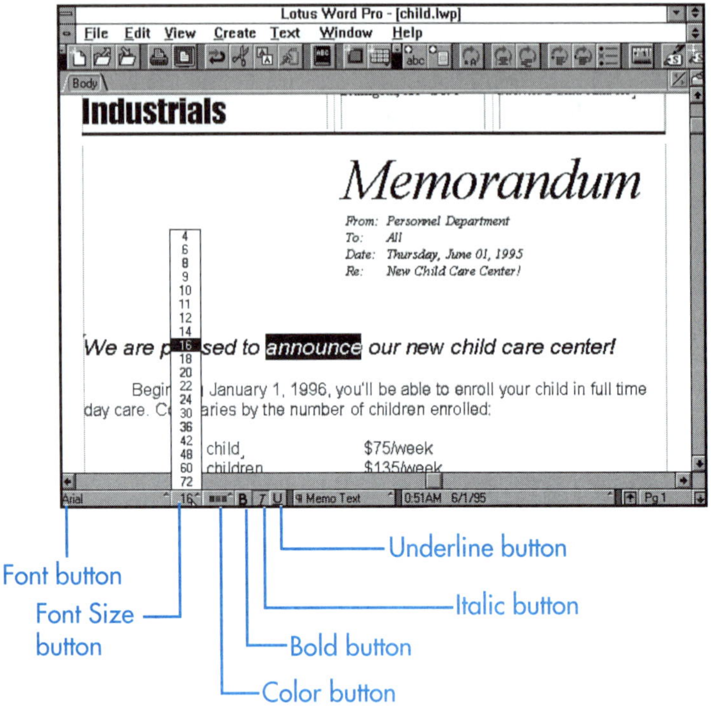

Figure 6.2 The Status bar provides a quick way to change text.

3. If necessary, make a further selection from the list or box that appears.

To change text with a cycle key, select the text and then cycle through a list of selections by pressing the key repeatedly until the text changes to the style you prefer. For example, to change the attributes of text, select it and press F5. The first time you press F5, the text is bolded. The next time, it is italicized. Keep pressing F5 to cycle through the list of available attributes. You can change the attributes associated with each cycle key; see Lesson 2 for help.

Table 6.1 lists the cycle keys related to text attributes and their purpose.

Table 6.1 The Cycle Keys Related to Text Attributes

Key	Function
F3	Changes the font of selected text
F4	Changes the point size of selected text
F5	Changes the attributes (such as bold, italic, and so on) of selected text

One Click Away You can also click on the Face Cycle (*face* is another word for font), Point Size Cycle, or Attribute Cycle SmartIcon to change text.

Copying Text Formatting

Fast Format is a convenient way to copy a text's attributes to other text. The attributes that are copied with Fast Format are combined with the receiving text's existing attributes. For example, if you use Fast Format to copy text that is Times New Roman 24 point bold onto text that is Arial 12 point italic, you'll end up with Times New Roman 24 point bold *italic* text.

Instead of copying text's attributes, you can copy its *style*. A text's style is a particular set of attributes that has been named and saved. Because you can add additional attributes to text that further define it beyond its style, Word Pro allows you to copy either this total combination of attributes or just the attributes associated with the style. You'll learn more about styles in Lesson 15.

To copy text attributes, follow these steps:

1. Place the cursor in the text whose attributes you want to copy.
2. Open the Text menu and select Fast Format, or press Ctrl+T. A dialog box appears, asking you to confirm which formats you want to make a copy of.

> **No Dialog?** If you select some text and then use the Fast format command, you won't see a dialog box because Word Pro assumes that you want to copy just the text's attributes, and not its style.

3. Click on the look of the text at the insertion point and then click on OK. The pointer changes to a paint-brush.
4. Select the text to change by dragging this brush over the text. (To change just a word, you don't have to drag over it; instead, you can simply click inside the word.) The text is changed to match the attributes you copied.
5. The pointer retains its brush shape, indicating that you can copy the saved attributes to other text, as well.
6. When you're done, press Esc to return to normal editing.

> **Not So Fast?** If you find that you use Fast Format a lot, you may want to add the Fast Format SmartIcon to the Text Iconbar. See Lesson 20 for more information.

In this lesson, you learned how to format selected text. You also learned how to copy text formatting. In the next lesson, you'll learn how to save and close files.

Lesson 7

Saving and Closing Files

In this lesson, you'll learn how to save your work and close files.

Saving a Document

You should always save your documents prior to exiting Word Pro because if you don't, you'll lose all your work! It's also a good idea to save a document periodically during a long work session. Why? Because if the PC is accidentally shut down, any unsaved work is lost. So *save your work often.*

> **Save Time!** Word Pro comes configured so that it periodically saves your work every 10 minutes. If you want to save your work more (or less) often, open the File menu and select User Setup. Then select Word Pro Preferences and click on the General tab. Then type the number of minutes between saves in the Automatically time save every xxxx minutes box and click on OK.

The first time you save a document, you must give it a name, so Word Pro displays a dialog box in which you can do just that. Later, when you tell Word Pro to resave your document, it does so without displaying a dialog box. To save your document, follow these steps:

1. Open the File menu and select Save, or click on the File Save SmartIcon. The dialog box shown in Figure

7.1 appears. (Note: If you've saved this document before, the file will be saved, but the dialog box will not appear.)

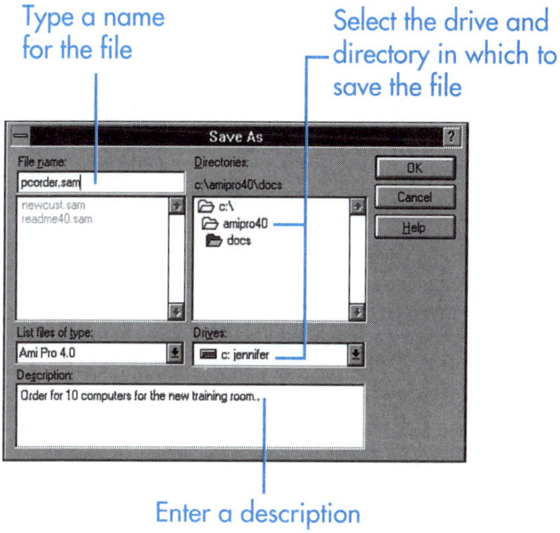

Figure 7.1 The Save As dialog box.

2. Select the drive and directory in which to save the file, or use the default, which saves your file in the \WORDPRO\DOCS directory.

3. Type a name for your document in the File name text box. You can use up to eight characters. Word Pro automatically adds a .LWP extension.

4. Type in a description for the document in the Description text box. You can use this description to identify the document later.

5. Click on OK, and Word Pro saves the document with the name you specified.

Oops, Same Name! If a file with the same name already exists, you're asked to verify if you want to overwrite the existing file. If you do, click on Yes. Otherwise, click on No and specify a different filename.

Once you save a document, it remains open on-screen so you can continue working on it. Or you can close the document if you wish (see the upcoming section on closing documents.) However, if you continue to work on a document, be sure to save it again before closing it.

Saving an Existing Document with a New Name or a Different File Format

After you save a file once, whenever you ask Word Pro to save the file again, it is simply saved to disk with the same name. To make a copy of a document under a different filename, you need to use the File Save As command.

In addition, when you save a file, Word Pro automatically saves it in Word Pro format. However, you can easily convert an existing document for use with another program with the File Save As command.

To save a copy of an existing file under a new filename or a different file format, follow these steps:

1. Open the File menu and select Save As. The File Save As dialog box appears (see Figure 7.2).
2. Select a new drive or directory in which to save the file, or use the default directory.
3. To save a copy of the document under a different name, type a new name for the file in the File name text box.

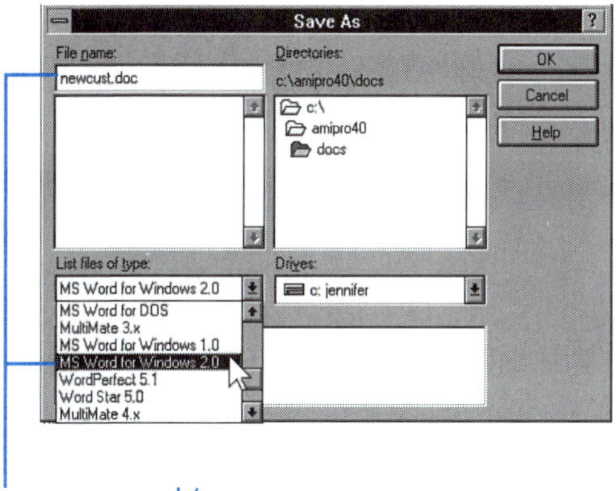

Select a different type and/or enter a new filename.

Figure 7.2 Select a different type and/or enter a new filename.

4. To save the file for use with a different program, select the desired file format from the List files of type drop-down list box.

What Gives? If you ask Word Pro to convert your document for use with another program, it may not be able to save all of the fancy formatting you had in the original document. However, basic formatting, such as alignment, font, and line spacing is saved.

5. Click on OK, and Word Pro saves the document with the new name and/or file format you specified.

Closing a Document

Closing a document removes it from the screen. You should always close a document whenever you finish working with it. That way, you can begin a new document or open an existing one without being distracted by a document you no longer need.

Just keep in mind that prior to closing a document, it's a good idea to save it.

To close a document, do the following:

1. Open the File menu.
2. Choose Close. If you made some changes to the document that you have not yet saved, you're given the opportunity to save it. Then Word Pro closes the current document. (If you have more than one document visible on-screen, the current document is the one with the darker title bar.)

Quick Close There are several ways to close a document. You can close the current document by opening the Window menu and selecting Close Window. You can also double-click on the document's Control Menu box (it looks like a tiny minus sign) located in the upper-left corner of the window, or you can press Ctrl+F4. To close all open documents, open the Window menu and select Close All Windows. Of course, when you exit Word Pro, all documents are closed automatically.

In this lesson, you learned how to save files in various ways. You also learned how to close a document when you're through with it. In the next lesson, you'll learn how to check your document for errors.

Lesson 8

Using Spell Check, Thesaurus, and Grammar Check

In this lesson, you'll learn how to check your document for errors with Word Pro's Spell Check, Grammar Check, and Format Check programs. You'll also learn how to use the Thesaurus to improve your vocabulary as you write.

Checking Your Spelling

You can check your spelling as you type, or after you finish a document. When you turn on Spell Check, it first marks any misspelled words currently in your document. If you leave the Spell Check bar open, Spell Check continues to mark misspelled words as you work. In addition, Spell Check uses a feature called SmartCorrect to automatically correct commonly misspelled words for you as you type them.

To turn on Spell Check, follow these steps:

1. Open the Edit menu and select Spell Check or click on the Spell Check SmartIcon. The Spell Check Bar appears at the top of the document window, as shown in Figure 8.1.

2. If you've already typed some text, Spell Check checks it for misspellings and highlights any misspelled words.

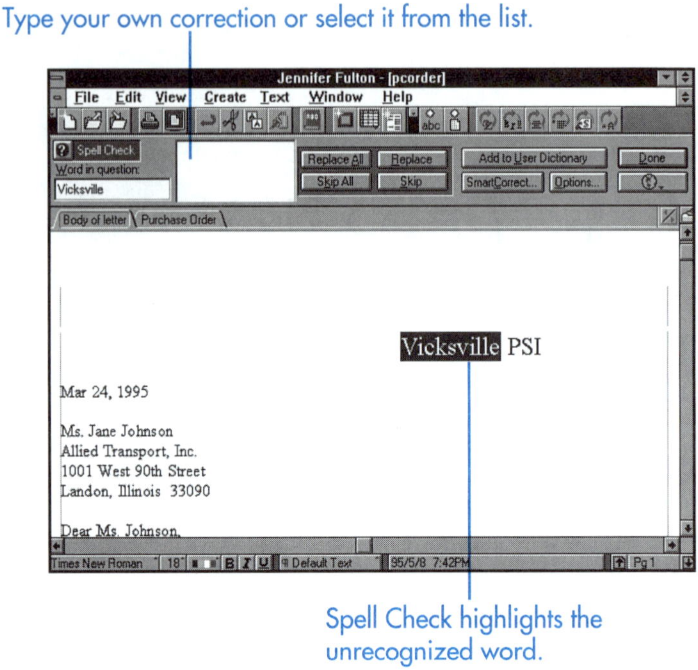

Figure 8.1 The Spell Check bar appears at the top of the window.

3. Correct a misspelled word by typing in the correct spelling or by choosing one of the following options:

 Replace All Replaces every occurrence of the unrecognized word with the word you select from the list.

 Replace Replaces just this occurrence of the unrecognized word with the word you select.

 Skip All Skips all occurrences of the unrecognized word.

 Skip Skips just this occurrence of the unrecognized word.

Add To User Dictionary Adds the unrecognized word to the permanent dictionary.

SmartCorrect Adds both the error and its correction to SmartCorrect. From now on, if you type the same error, it will automatically be replaced with the correction.

4. If you leave the Spell Check bar open as you work, it continues to mark any misspelled words until you turn it off. When you're through checking your spelling, remove the Spell Check bar by clicking on Done.

Clear Out If you've made your corrections and there are still some marked words that Spell Check just doesn't recognize (but are spelled correctly), clear the Spell Check marks by clicking on the Options button and selecting Clear Skipped Words.

Using the Thesaurus

Word Pro comes with an extensive Thesaurus that you can use to verify word definitions and find synonyms.

To use the Thesaurus, follow these steps:

1. Select the word for which you want to find a replacement.

2. Open the Edit menu and select Check Thesaurus. The Thesaurus dialog box shown in Figure 8.2 appears.

3. The word you selected in the document appears under **Looked up word**. Choose from the following options to find a replacement word:

   Meanings for Select from possible variations of the looked up word.

Synonyms for Select from alternatives to the word currently highlighted in the Meanings for list box.

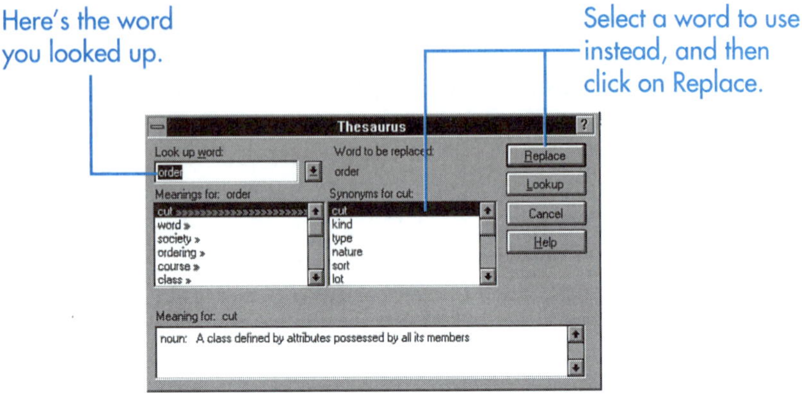

Figure 8.2 The Thesaurus dialog box offers many options.

4. To display additional alternatives for a selected word, click on Lookup. To return to the previous word you looked up, select it from the Looked up word drop-down list box.

5. Once you've selected a word that you want to use, click on Replace. The word you select replaces the word in the document that you started with.

6. To cancel the replacement operation and return to the document, click on Cancel.

Checking Your Grammar

Grammar Check checks your document for grammar problems. In this way, Grammar Check helps you improve your writing and clarify your meaning.

To use Grammar Check, do the following:

1. Move to the point in the document where you want to begin checking your grammar. To move to the beginning of the document, press Ctrl+Home.

2. Open the Edit menu and select Check Grammar. The Grammar Check review bar, shown in Figure 8.3, appears.

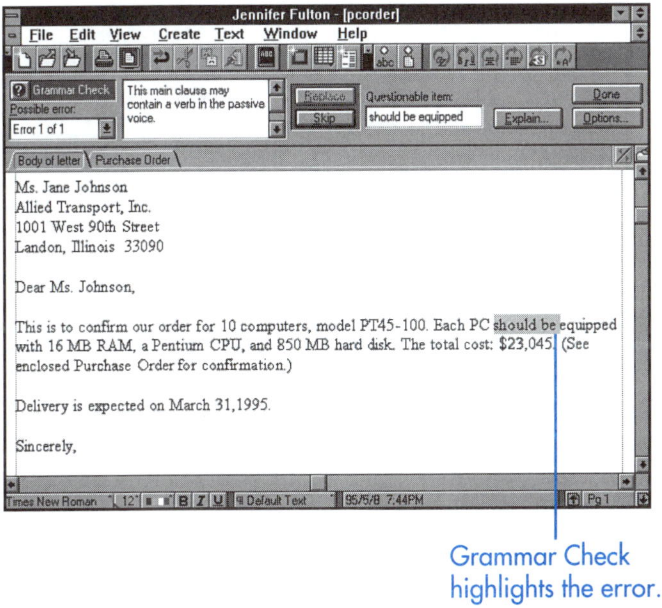

Figure 8.3 Use Grammar Check to improve your writing.

3. When Grammar Check finds an error, it highlights it. To correct the error, choose from these options:

   Skip Skips the error.

   Replace Replaces the error with the suggested fix.

You can also click in the document and manually correct the problem.

4. Grammar Check continues to check the rest of the document. Repeat step 3 for any additional errors.

5. When you're through checking the document for problems, click on Done. Grammar Check displays statistics that rate the readability of your document. Click on Close to return to the document window.

It Ain't Gooder If you don't like the way that Grammar Check proofs your document, you can change the rules. Just click on the Options button and change the Grammar check level or the Formality. Cancel a rule type by clicking on it. In addition, you can select other options by clicking on the Grammatical Style tab.

Completing a Format Check

Format Check can locate and correct common typing inconsistencies (such as two spaces between words), errors in style (such as margins that fluctuate), and sloppy bulleted lists.

You can have Format Check perform a quick check of your document or a more thorough one. Whichever you choose, you can always undo the changes Format Check makes if you find that you don't like them.

To use Format Check, follow these steps:

1. Move to the point in the document where you want to begin checking your format. To move to the beginning of the document, press Ctrl+Home.

2. Open the Edit menu and select Check Format. The Format Check dialog box appears.

3. Select the type of check you want to perform. If you want to, select from various checking options by clicking on the respective Options tab.

Another Option If you don't like the way that Format Check proofs your document, you can change this option as you go. Just click on the Options button on the Format Check review bar to redisplay the Options dialog box.

4. Click on OK. The Format Check review bar, shown in Figure 8.4, appears.

When Format Check finds an error, it displays a suggestion for fixing it.

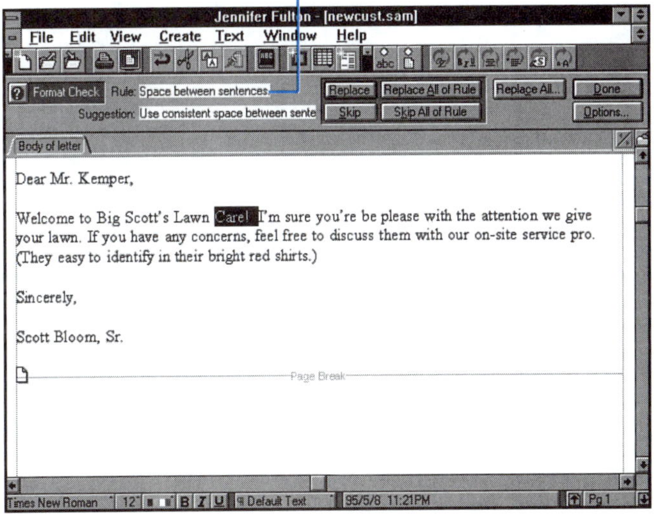

Figure 8.4 Format Check can correct common typing inconsistencies.

5. Format Check starts checking your document. When it finds an error, it displays the rule that was violated, along with a suggestion for fixing it. Choose from these options:

Replace Replaces the error with the suggested fix.

Replace All of Rule Replaces all errors of this type with the suggested fix.

Replace All Replaces all errors throughout the document with their suggested fixes. However, any rules you skipped earlier are ignored and not fixed.

Skip Skips this error.

Skip All of Rule Skips all occurrences of the current specific error.

6. Format Check continues to check the rest of the document. Repeat step 5 for any additional errors found.

7. When you're through checking the document for format errors, click on Done.

In this lesson, you learned how to verify the spelling of your documents. You learned how to use the Thesaurus to look for alternatives to words. You also learned how to use the Grammar Check to improve your meaning and Format Check to improve the look of your document. In the next lesson, you'll learn how to print your document.

Lesson 9

Printing Documents

In this lesson, you'll learn to customize the printing of your documents.

Printing the Current Document

Before you print your document, take the time to find and correct as many errors as possible. This process is called *proofing* your document—looking for errors in spelling, grammar, and formatting. For help in proofing your document before you print it, jump back to Lesson 8.

In addition to proofing your document, you might want to *preview* it. As you'll learn in Lesson 10, there are many ways to view a document, one of which is in Layout mode. Layout mode displays your document on-screen exactly as it will look when printed. Layout mode is the normal mode you work in with Word Pro, so to preview your document, you may not need to do anything. But if you skipped ahead and have been using another viewing mode, change back to Layout mode now, and preview your document before you print it.

When you're ready to print your document, do the following:

1. Open the File menu and select Print, or click on the Print SmartIcon. The Print dialog box shown in Figure 9.1 appears.

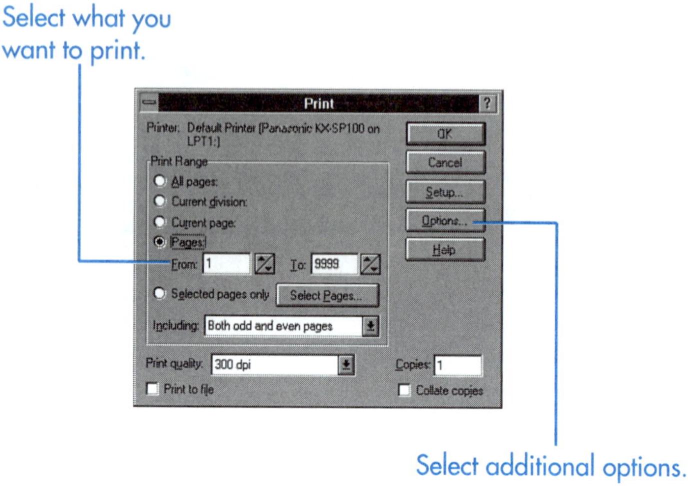

Figure 9.1 The Print dialog box.

2. Select an option from the Print Range area. You can print the entire document, the current division, the current page, or a range of pages. You can also select which pages to print by clicking on Select Pages and typing the page range you want to print. In addition, within the print range, you can print only odd pages, even pages, or both by selecting the appropriate option from the Including drop-down list.

3. Enter the number of copies you want to print in the Copies box.

Copy Cat! If you choose to print more than one copy of a document, you may want to select the Collate copies check box so that each copy prints in its entirety before the next copy. If you do not choose this option, Word Pro prints multiple copies of each page before printing the next page.

4. If you want to, select a different Print quality from the Print quality drop-down list.

5. To save your document for printing on another computer that doesn't have Word Pro, select the Print to file check box. You can then copy the file to a disk and take it to another PC for printing.

6. Printing your document in the background allows you to get back to your work much quicker. To use this option, just be sure that the Print this document in background option is selected. If you have a long document and you want to print it as quickly as possible, deselect this option.

7. To change any print options, click on the Options button. You'll learn about the printing options in the next section.

Changing Your Printer Setup You can change the printer setup by clicking on the Setup button. However, keep in mind that the changes you make here affect your Windows' printer options (and not just Word Pro's).

8. Click on OK, and the document begins printing.

Changing Printing Options

If you click on the Options button from within the Print dialog box, you can customize your print job with the additional options shown in Figure 9.2. Just select the options you want and then click on OK to return to the Print dialog box. Here are your options:

- **Reverse order** Prints the document, last page first, and so on.

- **Crop marks** Useful in typesetting, this option prints crop marks 1/2" outside of the margins.
- **Without pictures** This option prints only the actual text, without any pictures. The places where pictures would have appeared in the document are marked by boxes called *frames*.

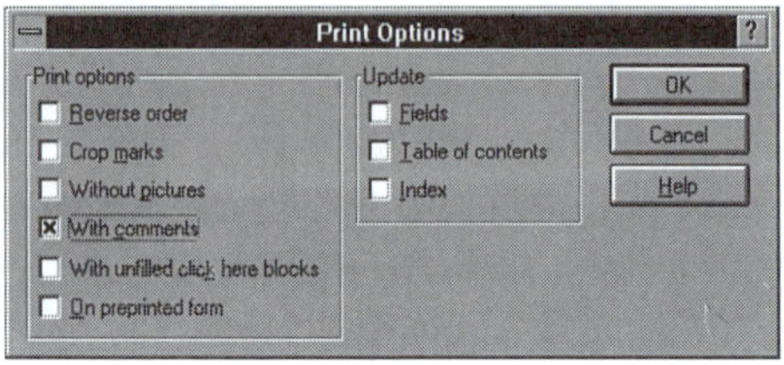

Figure 9.2 Word Pro lets you select from many print options.

Frames Frames are boxes that act as "holders" for text and graphics within a Word Pro document. You'll learn how to use frames in Lesson 21.

- **With comments** This option prints any comments that are attached to the document, along with the author's initials. Comments print at the end of a document.
- **With unfilled click here blocks** Prints all "click here" boxes, even if they were not used (filled with text or a graphic).
- **On preprinted form** Use this option when printing on preprinted forms, and Word Pro will not print certain additional information that you used when creating the document, such as lines and shades.

- **Update Fields, Table of contents,** and/or **Index** These options update the table of contents, the index, and the results of any *power fields*.

> **Power Fields** A power field is a dynamic tool you can use to update information in a document based on changing conditions, such as changing data, page numbers, figure references, and so on.

Printing in Landscape Mode

When you print a document, you can print it normally (Portrait mode) or in Landscape mode.

> **Landscape Mode** This means that the paper is oriented so that it is wider than it is long, as in 11" × 8 1/2." Portrait mode for the same size paper prints the document as 8 1/2" × 11."

> **Support Your Local Printer** In order to print a document in Landscape mode, your printer must support that option.

To print a document in Landscape mode, follow these steps:

1. Move to the beginning of the document by pressing Ctrl+Home.
2. Open the File menu and select Document Properties. Then select Page. The Page layout InfoBox appears, as shown in Figure 9.3.

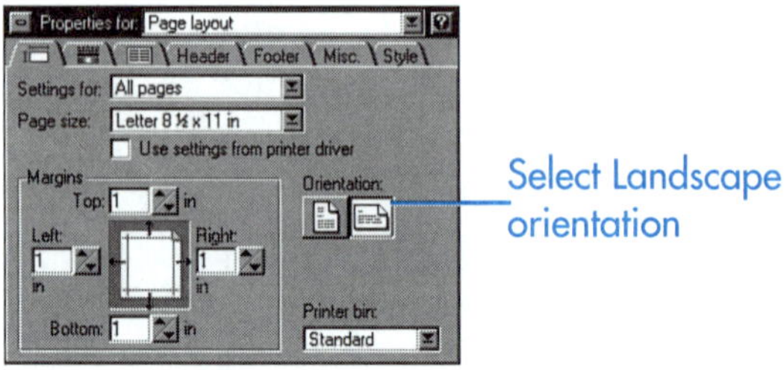

Figure 9.3 The Page layout InfoBox.

Fast Landscape To display the Page layout InfoBox quickly, right-click and select Page Properties from the pop-up menu.

3. Click on the Settings tab.
4. Under Orientation, click on the Landscape button.
5. Double-click on the Control-menu box to close the InfoBox and return to the document.
6. Click on the Print SmartIcon and then click on OK to print the document in Landscape mode.

Wide Open Range Word Pro prints the entire print range using the page orientation you specified in the Page layout InfoBox. If you need to print part of a document in Portrait mode and part in Landscape mode, you must first move to the point in the document where you want the new layout to begin, and then use the Insert Page Layout command from the Text menu. Click on Insert & Edit, and the Page layout InfoBox appears. Select Landscape orientation and then close the InfoBox.

Creating and Printing a Matching Envelope

With Word Pro, you can easily create a matching envelope for any letter. Of course, make sure that your printer is equipped to handle envelope printing (check your documentation). Just follow these steps:

1. Open the Create menu and select Other Document Part.

2. Select Envelope. Word Pro adds a new division to your document and displays the Envelope bar (see Figure 9.4).

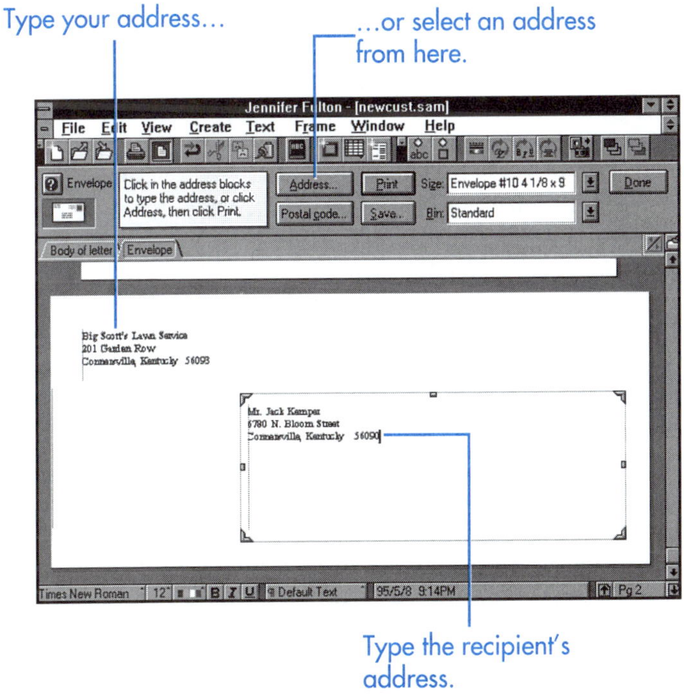

Figure 9.4 Creating envelopes is easy with the Envelope bar.

3. Click in the upper address block and type your address. (If you already had addresses in your letter, they should appear in the proper blocks, and you can just skip these two steps.)

4. Click in the lower address block and type the recipient's address.

Quick Address You can save an address permanently (such as your own) and reuse it as needed. Just click on the Address button, type the address you want to save and then click on Add Address to save it. Repeat for additional addresses. Later, click inside the block (frame) in which you want the address placed. Then click on the Address button and select the address you want to use from the list, and click on OK.

5. If necessary, change the Size of the envelope by selecting the appropriate option form the drop-down list.

6. To print just the envelope, click on Print. If you want to print the envelope when you print your document, click on Done. (To save the envelope in a separate file, click on Save.)

You can print a postal code mark at the bottom of the envelope if you want to by clicking on the Postal code button, selecting a bar code, and then clicking on OK.

In this lesson, you learned how to print your documents. You also learned about various printing options, including how to print in Landscape mode. In addition, you learned how to create and print an envelope. In the next lesson, you'll learn how to change your view of a document.

Lesson 10

Viewing a Document

In this lesson, you will learn to work with your Word Pro documents more effectively by choosing the correct viewing option.

Choosing the Correct Display View

Word Pro provides many options for viewing your document. The different display views control how much of the document is displayed on your screen at one time. There are three display views:

Layout This view displays your document as it will look when printed. It is the most common viewing mode.

Draft This view displays only text (and no frames, graphics, headers, footers, etc.) Working with text only allows you to work faster, since Word Pro isn't wasting time trying to display fancy graphics, etc.

Page Sorter Use this view to display all the pages in your document. This view makes it easy to reorganize a large document.

To change your display view:

1. Open the View menu.
2. Select either Layout, Draft, or Page Sorter. Page Sorter view is shown in Figure 10.1.

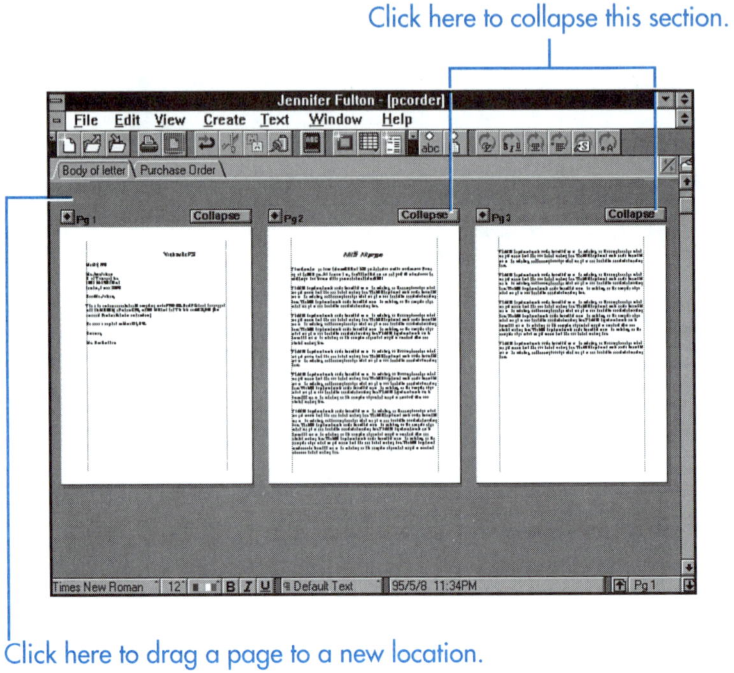

Figure 10.1 Page Sorter view allows you to easily reorganize your document.

Hey, Where Are My Pages? If you don't see all the pages in your document, click on the Expand button to display all your pages. Then you can click on any Collapse button to collapse (hide) that page. To reorganize your document, just drag a page wherever you want and "drop" it.

Setting the Zoom Level

Sometimes you'll want to "back off" and look at the whole page, and other times, you want to zoom in and examine a specific area of the document. With Word Pro, you have the flexibilty to view your document however you need to.

The most common zoom level is 100 percent, which allows you to see your text easily. However, you won't see both the left and right margins in this view. To solve this problem, you can zoom to margin width or page width (which zooms out to the margins or the edge of the page). You can also zoom to full page, to display the current page in its entirety. And of course, you can zoom to any percentage between these standard zoom levels.

To change the zoom:

1. Open the View menu.
2. To zoom to 100 percent or Full Page, select that option off the menu. To select a different standard zoom, click on Zoom To and make your selection, such as 75 percent.

To zoom to a non-standard percentage, change the custom level: click on Zoom To, then select Other. Change the Custom level to the desired percentage and click on OK.

Zoom Zoom You can switch between the two most common views, 100 percent and Full Page, by clicking on the Full Page SmartIcon. Click once to zoom to Full Page, then click again to zoom back to 100 percent.

Using the Special Views

Word Pro comes with four special views that combine the various viewing modes and zoom levels to create a unique working environment. You can edit within any of these windows, and even drag and drop text between them. You can also adjust the sizes of the various windows by dragging the split bar. (If you're not sure what a split bar is, see Lesson 11 for help.)

PageWalker Combines the Layout and Full Page views.

Panorama Provides a full-width Layout view and a four page view. (See Figure 10.2.)

DocSkimmer Combines an outline and a multi-page view with Draft view.

Zoomer Provides a Layout and a Draft view, along with a multi-page view for jumping around a document.

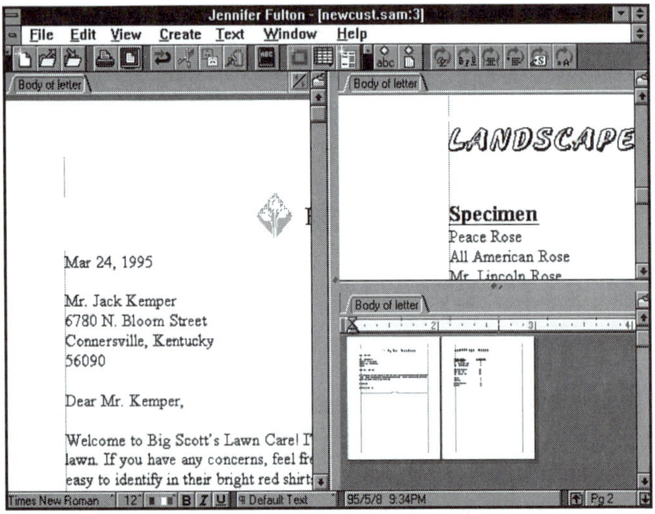

Figure 10.2 Panorama is just one of the special views.

To select a special view:

1. Open the View menu and select Special Views. The Special Views dialog box appears.
2. Select the view you want.
3. Click on OK.

What's This? To switch views, be sure to remove the old view first, or Word Pro will try to combine them. To remove a special view, open the View menu and select Clear All Splits.

Controlling What's Displayed On-Screen

Normally, the division tabs, the Status bar, the SmartIcons, and the scroll bars appear on-screen. You can easily remove these items to have more room to work in. You can also add more items on the screen, to make it easier to perform certain tasks. For example, you can display the Ruler to make it easier to set tabs and change the margins.

To display (or not display) an item on-screen:

1. Open the View menu and select Show/Hide.
2. Select the item you wish to display or hide. (Items that are currently displayed are marked with a checkmark. Selecting them again causes them to be removed from the screen.)

If you want to remove all items from the screen so you have the largest area in which to work, use the Clean Screen option:

1. Open the View menu and select Show/Hide.
2. Select Clean Screen. Your document is displayed on a clean screen, as shown in Figure 10.3.
3. To return to a normal viewing screen, click on the Leave Clean Screen icon.

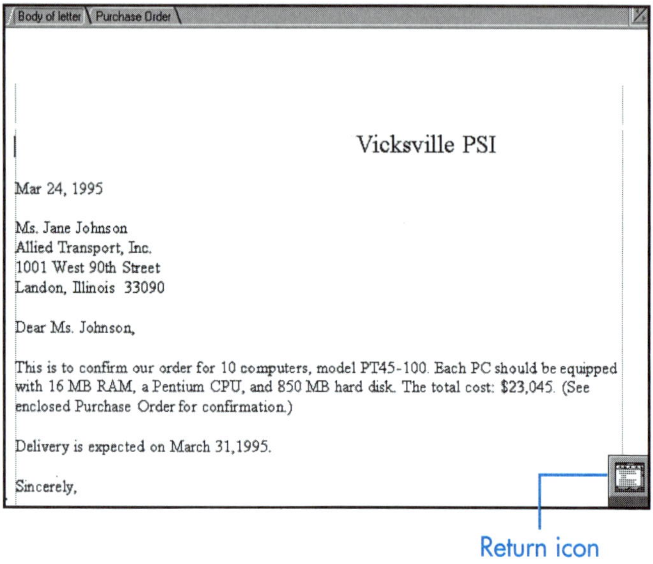

Figure 10.3 To create the largest work area, use Clean Screen.

You can set your viewing preferences to reflect what you normally like to have displayed on-screen. This saves you having to customize your view each time.

To set your viewing preferences:

1. Open the View menu and select Set View Preferences. The View Preferences dialog box, shown in Figure 10.4, appears.
2. If necessary, click on the Show tab.
3. Select the items you wish to display on a regular basis.
4. Click on OK.

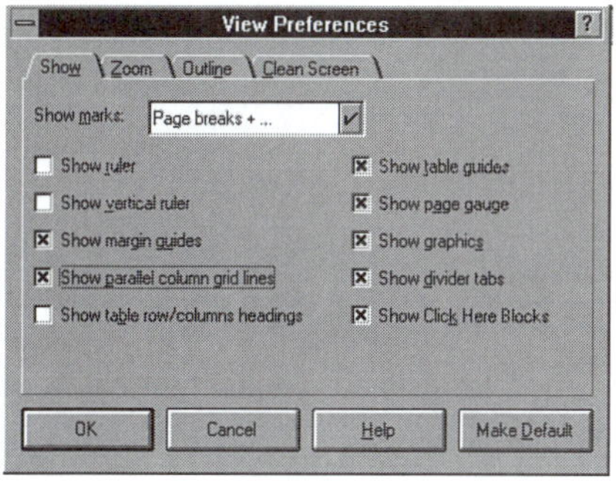

Figure 10.4 The Set View Preferences dialog box.

In this lesson, you learned how to control the way your document is displayed on the screen. In the next lesson, you will learn how to work with multiple document windows.

Lesson 11

Using Multiple Windows

In this lesson, you will learn to edit multiple documents at the same time. You will also learn how you can open the same document in multiple windows.

Viewing Multiple Documents

There are times when you edit a document and you want to view another document as well. For example, you may want to copy or move data from one document to another. Or perhaps you need to reference information in one document as you edit another. In any case, the ability to simultaneously view multiple documents is sometimes important. Here you will learn how to arrange open documents on-screen.

To open another document while you're working on your current document, use the File Open SmartIcon. Or, if you prefer, you can open a new document with the File New SmartIcon instead. Once you open another document window, Word Pro automatically maximizes it. You can then arrange your document windows so that you can view them all.

You can arrange multiple windows in two special ways—*tiling* or *cascading*. In addition, windows can be tiled left to right, or top to bottom.

Tiling and Cascading Windows Tiling two or more windows causes them to be arranged vertically across the screen, like columns. Windows can also be tiled from top to bottom. Cascading two or more windows arranges them diagonally, from the upper left to lower right corners of the screen. Cascading windows overlap slightly.

Figures 11.1 and 11.2 show tiled and cascaded windows.

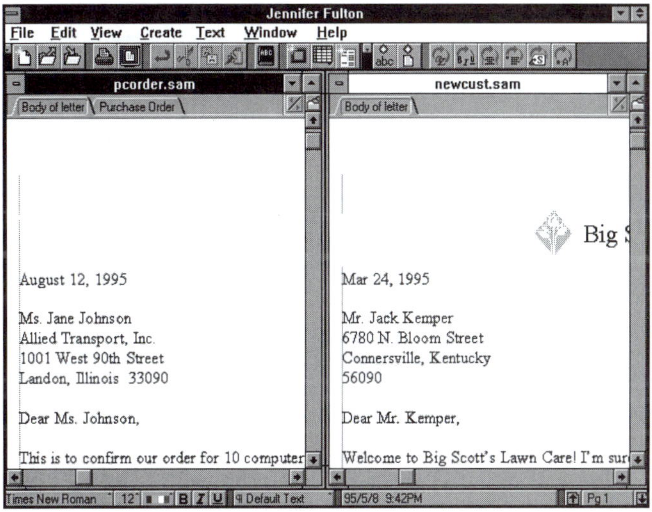

Figure 11.1 Tiled windows share equal space on the screen.

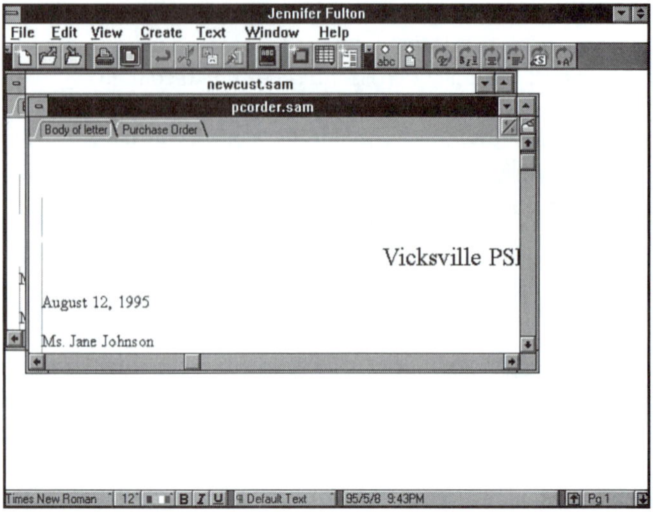

Figure 11.2 Cascaded windows run diagonally down the screen.

To arrange document windows in a tiled fashion:

1. Open the documents you want to view.
2. Open the Window menu.
3. Choose Tile Left-Right or Tile Top-Bottom. Word Pro tiles the open windows.

To arrange document windows in a cascaded fashion:

1. Open the documents you want to view.
2. Open the Window menu.
3. Choose Cascade. Word Pro cascades the open windows.

Once you arrange your windows to your liking, you can switch between windows in several ways. If the window you want to switch to is visible, simply click on any portion of that window, and it becomes the active window. If the window is not visible, select the window to switch to from the listing which appears at the end of the Window menu.

Displaying the Same Document in Two Windows

When working with larger documents, you'll often find that you need to view different parts of a document at the same time. Thankfully, Word Pro gives you the flexibility to split your document into multiple windows so you can view different parts of it at the same time.

To display a document in two windows:

1. Open the View menu.
2. Choose Split Left-Right or Split Top-Bottom. Figure 11.3 shows a document split top-bottom.

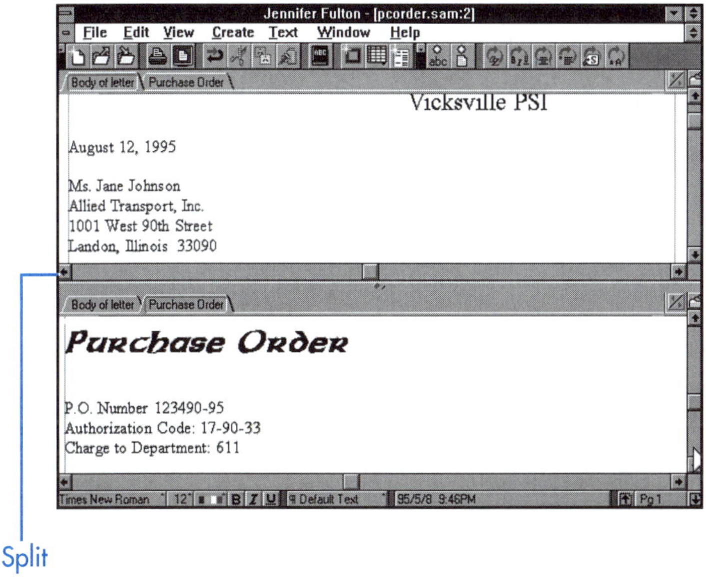

Figure 11.3 A split allows you to see two parts of the same document.

Now that your document is displayed in two windows, you can adjust the size of each window by moving the split. To adjust the split, click on it and drag it to its new location. Release the mouse button and the window is resplit.

To remove the split and return to a normal viewing window, open the View menu and select Clear All Splits.

Do the Splits You can view your document in several custom viewing formats with Special Views. Each special view makes use of splits and various viewing modes to create a unique working environment. See Lesson 10 for help.

In addition, you can change the view of the document within each window (see Lesson 10). You can even split a window further by clicking in that window to activate it, and repeating the steps above.

In this lesson, you learned how to open multiple documents for editing and viewing. You also learned how to arrange multiple windows for the same document. In the next lesson, you will learn how to format paragraphs.

Lesson 12 Formatting Paragraphs

In this lesson, you will learn to format your paragraphs by changing alignment, indentation, line spacing, lines, and shadows.

Changing Alignment and Indentation

Although you can adjust the alignment and indentation of a paragraph, you may prefer to change the settings for the paragraph style. Changing the alignment or indentation of a paragraph style automatically changes all of the paragraphs in that style, at one time. In this lesson, you will learn how to change the settings for a selected paragraph. You will learn how to modify paragraph styles in Lesson 15.

> **Alignment** Alignment refers to the way that text is placed between margins.

> **Indentation** The indent is an extra "space" between the edge of a paragraph and the margin.

Word Pro supports left, right, center, and full justified alignment. Left aligned text is similar to the text in this book—it always "touches" the left margin. Figure 12.1 shows examples of each kind of alignment.

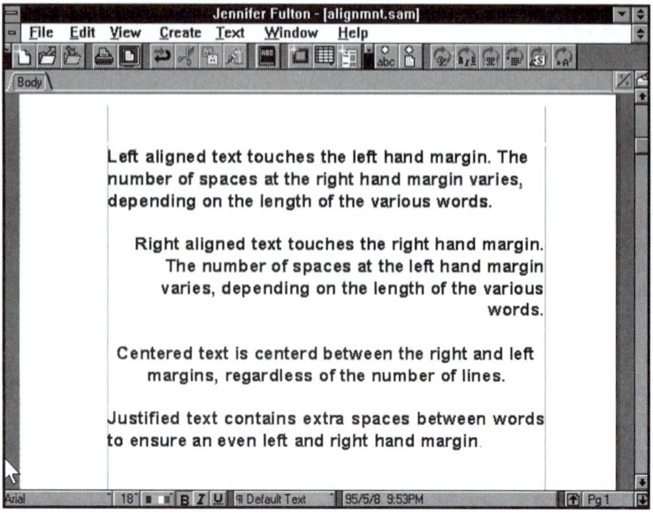

Figure 12.1 Word Pro offers many choices for aligning text.

To change the alignment of selected paragraphs:

1. Select the paragraphs you want to change. If you want to change only one paragraph, just click within it.
2. Open the Text menu and select Alignment.
3. Choose the alignment you prefer: Left, Right, Center, or Full Justify. Word Pro aligns the paragraph as specified.

Get in Line You can quickly align text with the Alignment Cycle SmartIcon. Just click repeatedly until you cycle to the type of alignment you desire. You can also press F6 to cycle alignment.

Indentation refers to how far text is placed from the left or right margins. You can indent all the lines of a paragraph, a specified amount from the left margin, or from both the left and right margins. You can also indent only the first line of a paragraph, or all the lines *but the first line.*

To change the indentation of selected paragraphs:

1. Select the paragraphs whose indent you want to change.
2. Right-click and select Text Properties from the pop-up menu. The Text InfoBox appears.
3. Click on the Alignment tab. (See Figure 12.2.)

Quick Change Artist Note that you can change a paragraph's alignment, line spacing, and other characteristics with the Text InfoBox. So if you have many changes to make, use the Text InfoBox rather than the Text menu to make your changes.

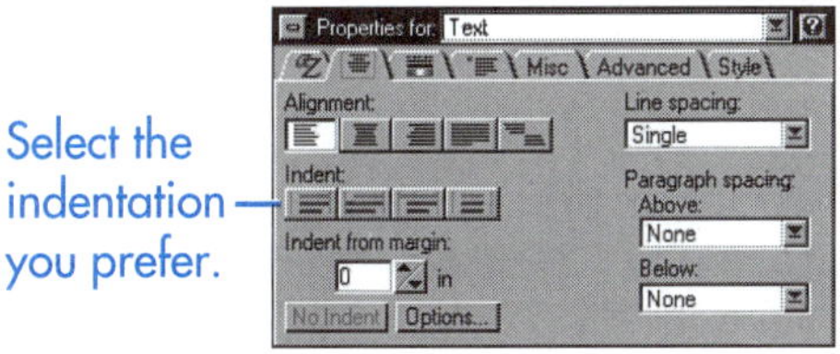

Figure 12.2 The Text InfoBox allows you to quickly change indentation.

4. Choose the indentation you prefer.
5. By default, the indent is set to .5 inches from the left margin. You can increase or decrease this amount as desired under Indent from margin. For more fine-tuning options, click on the Options button.

But I Don't Like It! To remove an indent, click on the No Indent button.

6. Close the Text InfoBox when you're through.

Making a 'Dent You can quickly indent text by pressing F7 to indent all lines of a paragraph .5 inch. You can add other indentation types to the cycle key; see Lesson 2 for help.

Adjusting Line Spacing

You may want to adjust the line spacing (such as single or double spacing) for sections of text in order to aid in proofreading, create a visual contrast, or make it more readable.

Although you can adjust the line spacing of selected paragraphs, you may prefer to change the settings for the paragraph style. Changing the line spacing of a paragraph style automatically changes all of the paragraphs in that style, at one time. You will learn how to modify paragraph styles in Lesson 15.

To adjust the line spacing for selected paragraphs:

1. Select the paragraphs whose line spacing you want to change.
2. Right-click and select Text Properties from the pop-up menu that appears.
3. Click on the Alignment tab.
4. Select the line spacing you prefer from the Line spacing drop-down list box.
5. Close the Text InfoBox when you're through.

Leading Leading is one of the options under Line spacing. Leading is the amount of space between the bottom of one line of text and another. Leading changes based on the current point size of text. If text is set to 12 points and you set leading to 14, then the space between the lines of text is roughly 2 points. If you change the text to 14 points, the leading becomes 16 points to maintain this 2 point difference.

Adjusting the Spacing Between Paragraphs

In addition to setting line spacing, you can adjust the amount of spacing which precedes or follows selected paragraphs if you want. For example, you can specify additional spacing after a heading. Again, you might find this option more useful when applied to a style, which allows you to change multiple paragraphs at once. For example, instead of changing one heading, you could change the heading style and end up changing all your headings in one step. You'll learn how to change style settings in Lesson 15.

To adjust the paragraph spacing for selected paragraphs:

1. Select the paragraphs whose spacing you want to change.
2. Right-click and select Text Properties from the pop-up menu that appears.
3. Click on the Alignment tab in the Text InfoBox.
4. From the Above and Below drop-down list boxes, select the amount of spacing you want to precede or follow the selected paragraphs.
5. Close the Text InfoBox when you're through.

Adding Lines and Shadows around Paragraphs

To draw the eye to a specific paragraph, add lines or shadows around it. With lines and shadows, you can enchance reports by highlighting important information. (See Figure 12.3.)

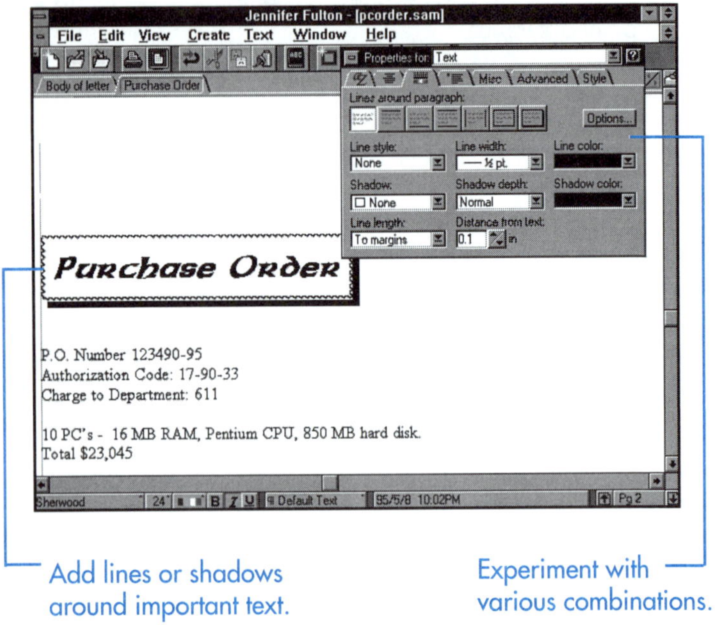

Figure 12.3 Adding lines and shadows can enhance the look of your document.

You can add a line on any side of a paragraph, or you can completely surround it. In addition, you can select from several shadow styles.

To add lines or shadows to selected paragraphs:

1. Select the paragraphs to which you want to add lines or shadows.

2. Right-click and select Text Properties from the pop-up menu that appears.

3. Click on the Lines and Colors tab in the Text InfoBox.

4. Select a line or shadow option under Lines around paragraph.

5. If you want, change the Line style, Line width, and/or Line color.

6. If you select the shadow option in step 4, select a different style under Shadow if you want. Make additional selections under Shadow depth and/or Shadow color.

7. To control the area around which the lines appear, make a selection under Line length and Distance from text.

8. Close the Text InfoBox when you're through.

Keeping Paragraphs Together

You can instruct Word Pro to keep particular paragraphs together on the same page, to keep the text for an entire paragraph on the same page, or to insert a page break before or after certain paragraphs. In addition, you can control whether the normal paragraph spacing occurs when that paragraph falls at the end of a page. These features are useful when creating newsletters and reports, especially when you have captions and figures which relate to particular paragraphs.

To set these paragraph options:

1. Select the paragraphs whose formatting you want to change.

2. Right-click and select Text Properties from the pop-up menu that appears.

3. Click on the Advanced tab in the Text InfoBox. (See Figure 12.4.)

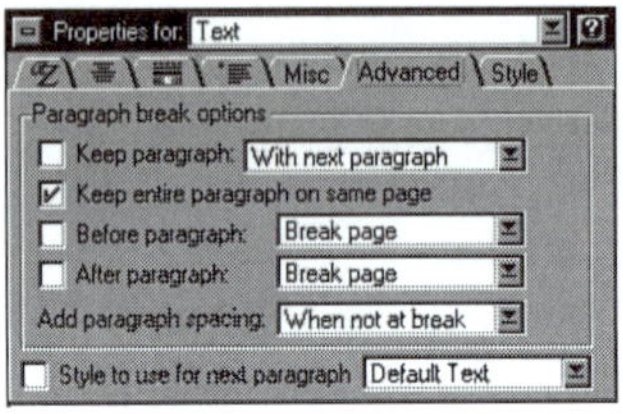

Figure 12.4 Control the page on which paragraphs appear with the Advanced dialog.

4. Select from among the various options.

5. Close the Text InfoBox when you're through.

In this lesson, you learned how to format your paragraphs. In the next lesson, you'll learn how to create bulleted and numbered lists.

Lesson 13

Creating Bulleted and Numbered Lists

In this lesson, you'll learn how to place bullets or numbers in front of paragraphs in order to create lists.

Creating a Bulleted List

A bulleted list is useful for listing similar items, such as the features of a popular product, the benefits of a new procedure, or the characteristics of a prospective employee. For example, to list the benefits of Word Pro, you might create a list like this:

- SmartMasters make documents easy to create
- InfoBoxes provide fast access to formatting tools
- Complete proofing tools give your documents a professional look

To create a bulleted list, follow these steps:

1. Right-click in the document you want to contain the bulleted list and select Text Properties from the pop-up menu. The Text InfoBox appears.
2. Click on the Bullets tab (see Figure 13.1).

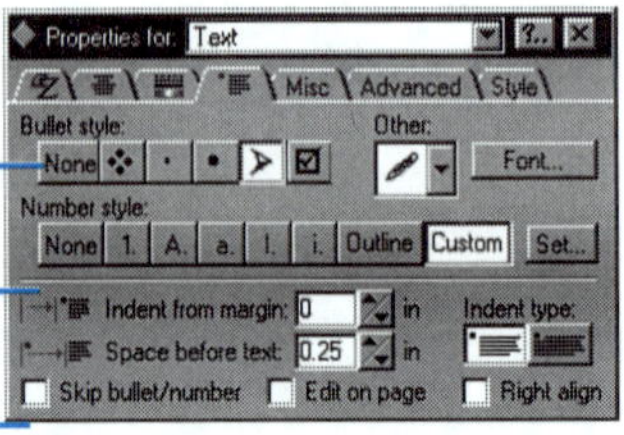

Figure 13.1 Word Pro provides a variety of bullets to choose from.

3. Click a button on the Bullet style bar to select a bullet style.

> **But I Don't See Anything I Like!** You can customize a button with a different bullet by clicking on the Font button, selecting a font, and then selecting a bullet from the Other list.

4. If you want to, you can adjust the amount of space between the bullet and the text by entering a new amount in the Space before text text box.
5. Adjust the indentation by changing the amount in the Indent from margin text box and by selecting one of the Indent type options.
6. Click in the document and type your bulleted list.
7. To discontinue the bullets and return to regular text, click on the None button under Bullet style.

> **Skip a Beat** To skip the bullet for one paragraph, select the Skip bullet/number check box. Word Pro remembers your selections and resumes with the same bullet style when you select the Skip bullet/number check box.

8. Close the Text InfoBox when you're through by double-clicking its Control-menu box.

If you want to transform an existing list into a bulleted list, just select it, then follow these steps. You can also create a bulleted list by selecting a bulleted list style from the Status bar and then typing text, or by selecting it first.

Creating a Numbered List

A numbered list is useful for enumerating steps, such as the steps in a complex procedure. I've used numbered lists throughout this book to show you the steps to complete a particular task. You can also use a numbered list to list items by priority, such as a top ten list.

To create a numbered list, follow these steps:

1. Right-click in the document you want to contain the numbered list and select Text Properties from the pop-up menu. The Text InfoBox appears.

2. Click on the Bullets tab (see Figure 13.2).

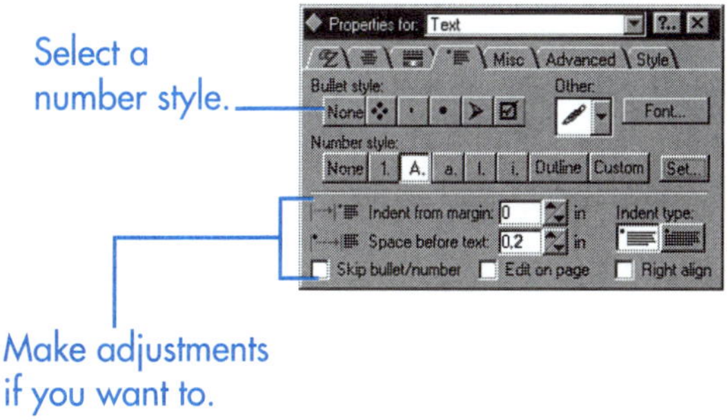

Figure 13.2 Word Pro provides several number styles.

3. Click a button on the Number style bar to select a number style.

But I Don't Want to Start with One! To change the starting number, click on the Set button and change the Start at setting. Click on OK to return to the Bullets tab.

4. If you want to add some text before or after the number, click on Custom, and the Numbered List Options box appears. Add your text and click on OK to return to the Bullets tab.
5. If you want to, you can adjust the amount of space between the number and the text by changing the amount in the Space before text text box.
6. Adjust the indentation by changing the amount in the Indent from margin text box and by selecting one of the Indent type options.
7. Click in the document and type your numbered list.
8. To discontinue the numbered list and return to regular text, click on the None button under Number style.

Skip a Beat To skip numbering for one paragraph, select the Skip bullet/number check box. Word Pro remembers your selections and resumes with the same numbered list style when you select the Skip bullet/number check box.

9. Close the Text InfoBox when you're through by double-clicking its Control-menu box.

If you have an existing list which you want to turn into a numbered list, you can—just select it and then follow the steps here.

In this lesson, you learned how to create bulleted and numbered lists. In the next lesson, you'll learn how to change the formatting of a page.

Lesson 14

Changing the Page Layout

In this lesson, you'll learn how to modify the layout of a page by changing its margins, size, and orientation, as well as adding borders, shadows, and page numbers.

A Word About Page Layout

Just as paragraph styles are predefined formats for paragraphs, *page layouts* are predefined formats for the pages in a document. You can adjust the settings of the master page layout, thereby affecting all of the pages in your document, or you can insert additional page layouts into your document for specific pages.

> **How Can I Be Sure I'm Affecting All Pages?** Whenever you use the Page layout InfoBox (as explained throughout this lesson), you're affecting all the pages in your document, *regardless* of what page you're currently on. If you want to affect only some pages, see the section "Inserting a New Page Layout," later in this lesson.

Changing Page Margins

There are four margins on every page: one each at the top, bottom, left, and right sides of the page. The *margin* is the open space between the edge of the paper and the beginning of the text. Additional space may be added between the margin and the text along the left and right sides; this extra space is called an *indent*. (You learned about indents and how to set them in Lesson 12.)

Although most page layout settings affect all the pages in your document, Word Pro allows you the freedom of setting margins for just the left (even numbered) or right (odd numbered) pages in a document. You can also set the margins for mirror pages, where the margins for left and right pages are the same, only opposite (mirrored), like in a book.

To change the page margins, follow these steps:

1. Right-click and select Page Properties from the pop-up menu. The Page layout InfoBox appears.
2. Click on the Settings tab (see Figure 14.1).

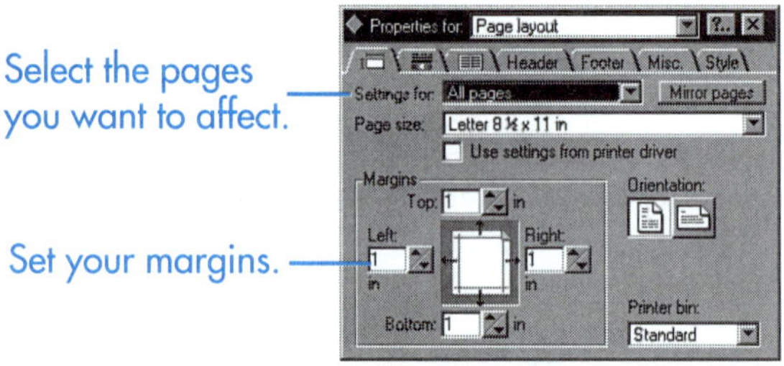

Figure 14.1 Set your margains. Select the pages you want to affect.

3. Select the pages you want to affect from the Settings for the drop-down list.
4. Change the settings for top, bottom, left, and right margins as desired by adjusting the numbers in their corresponding text boxes in the Margins area.
5. Close the Page layout InfoBox by double-clicking its Control-menu box.

Adjusting the Paper Size and Page Orientation

Word Pro provides many standard paper sizes to choose from, including 8 1/2 × 11 inches and 8 1/2 × 14 inches. In addition, you can create your own custom paper size.

On the other hand, there are only two different kinds of page orientations: *Portrait* and *Landscape*. Portrait orientation is normal, where text is printed on a page across its narrow side, as with an 8 1/2 × 11-inch piece of paper. Landscape orientation prints text along the page's widest side, as with 11 × 8 1/2-inch paper.

To change the paper size and/or page orientation, follow these steps:

1. Right-click and select Page Properties from the pop-up menu. The Page layout InfoBox appears.
2. Click on the Settings tab (see Figure 14.1).
3. Select a paper size from the Page size drop-down list.

Getting through Custom To create a custom paper size, select Custom from the Page size list. Then enter the size measurements in the Custom Page Size dialog box and click on OK.

4. If you want, select a different Orientation by clicking on the appropriate button.
5. Close the Page layout InfoBox by double-clicking on its Control-menu box.

Adding Page Borders and Shadows

You can add a border and/or a shadow around the edges of your pages if you like. The effect can be quite dramatic, so you might want to limit this effect to a special page such as the title page for a report. To limit the pages these settings affect, see the section "Inserting a New Page Layout," later in this lesson.

To add page borders or shadows, follow these steps:

1. Right-click and select Page Properties from the pop-up menu. The Page layout InfoBox appears.
2. Click on the Lines and Colors tab (see Figure 14.2).

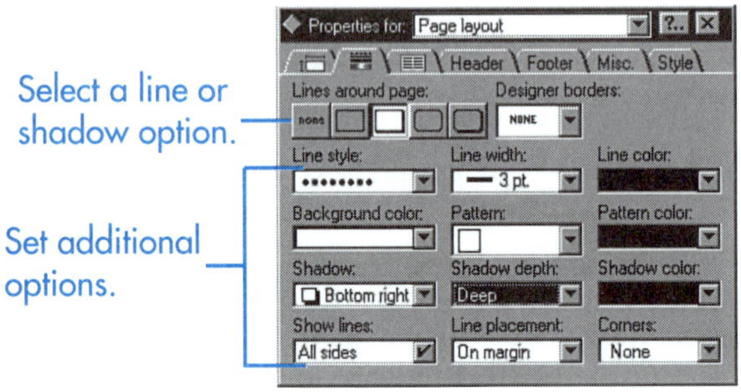

Figure 14.2 Add lines and shadows to your pages.

3. Click a line or shadow option under Lines around page.
4. If you want to, you can change the Line style, Line width, and/or Line color by selecting a different option from the appropriate drop-down list.
5. Fill your pages with color (or shading) by selecting a Background color, Pattern, and Pattern color from the corresponding drop-down lists.
6. If you select a shadow option in step 3, select a different style from the Shadow drop-down list if you want to. Make additional selections from the Shadow depth and/or Shadow color drop-down lists as necessary.

7. To control on which sides the border lines appear, make a selection from the Show lines drop-down list box. To control where the border lines appear, select an option from the Line placement drop-down list box. To adjust the corners of the border, make a selection from the Corners drop-down list box.

8. Close the Page layout InfoBox by double-clicking on its Control-menu box.

Adding Page Numbers

With Word Pro, you'll add page numbers to a document within the header or a footer because it gives you precise control over where the page number prints on the page, and on which pages. A *header* appears at the top of the pages in a document, whereas a *footer* appears at the bottom. The header or the footer usually includes more information than just the page number, such as the name of the current section, the title of the report, the author of the document, and so on.

Each document contains an invisible header and footer area built-in; you don't have to use this area at all—if you don't use it, it doesn't print. However, if you want to number your pages, you do need to use the header or footer area. (You'll learn more about headers and footers in Lesson 18.)

Just follow these steps:

1. Click inside the header or the footer area. If you can't see a header or footer, open the View menu, select Show/Hide, and then select Headers & Footers. It doesn't matter what page you're on, since, like all the other page options, the default is to affect all pages within the document.

2. Position the cursor where you want the page number to appear, then open the Text menu and select Insert Page Number. The Insert Page Number dialog box appears, as shown in Figure 14.3.

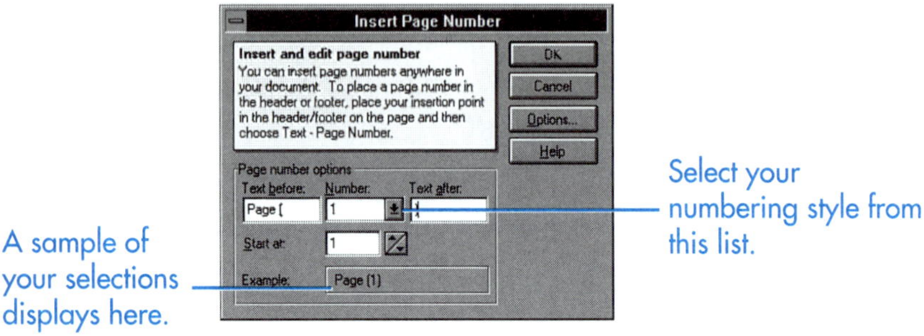

Figure 14.3 The Insert Page Number dialog box.

3. If you want text to appear before or after the number, type it in the Text before or Text after boxes. For example, type the word **Page** in the Text before box.

4. If you want to use something other than numbers to organize your pages, select that numbering method from the Number drop-down list. For example, you could number your pages with I, II, III, or a, b, c, and so on.

5. If you want to start with a different number other than 1, adjust the Start at value.

6. If you want to start numbering on page 2 (to skip a title page, for example), click on Custom. Select the page number to start on from the Begin numbering on page list. You can also reset page numbers with each section or division and even include the section/division name if you want. Click on OK to return to the Settings tab.

Inserting a New Page Layout

To override the master page layout for selected pages, you need to insert a new page layout. The settings you specify in this new layout will be in effect for the rest of the pages in the document, unless you insert another page layout on some later page.

For example, you could insert a page layout on page 6 so that you could create a header or footer that's different than the one on pages 1 through 5. Or you could change the page orientation to Landscape, beginning with page 6.

Place Settings Precise placement is necessary when inserting page layouts, so be sure the insertion point is at the top of a page before inserting a new page layout.

To insert a new page layout, follow these steps:

1. Move to the page on which you want to start a new page layout.
2. Open the Text menu and select Insert Page Layout. The Insert Page Layout dialog box appears, as shown in Figure 14.4.

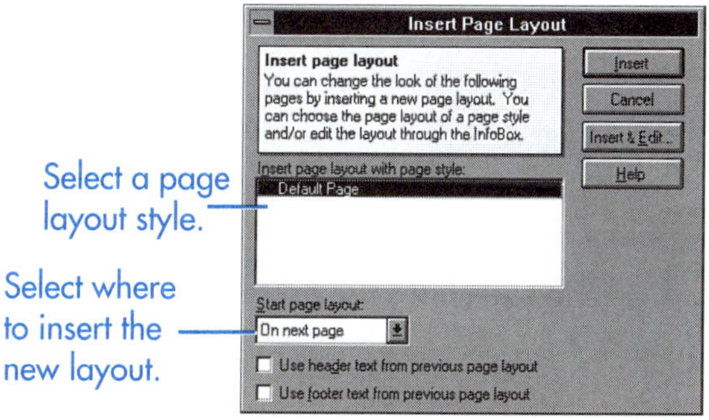

Figure 14.4 The Insert Page Layout dialog box.

3. Select the page style you want to insert from the Insert page layout with page style list box.

No Style? Word Pro only comes with one page style, but you can create your own page styles for reuse in other documents with the Style tab of the Page layout InfoBox. See Lesson 15 for help in creating a style.

4. Select where you want the new page layout to start from the Start page layout list. To start on this page, select the Within page option.
5. If you want to retain the same header and/or footer that appears on previous pages, select either the Use header text from previous page layout or Use footer text from previous page layout check box.
6. Click Insert, and a page layout mark (which looks like a page icon followed by the text, Page Style: xxxxx) appears. If you want to make changes to the page layout, click Insert & Edit instead, and you'll be taken to the Page layout InfoBox.

To remove a page layout, just select the page layout mark and press Delete.

In this lesson, you've learned how to modify the page layout for all or selected pages. In the next lesson, you'll learn how to use styles.

Lesson 15

Using Styles

In this lesson, you'll learn how to use styles: how to create and change them, and how to assign a style to text.

What Is a Style?

In a newspaper or a magazine, it's easy to see how parts of the layout are given a standardized look. Headlines, subheads, the text of each article, figure captions, and even where the page numbers go are standardized, to give such documents a look of consistency.

In Word Pro, you use styles to give your documents this same look of consistency. A *style* defines the characteristics of a paragraph, such as its font, point size, alignment, line spacing, and so on. So rather than painstakingly formatting every paragraph, you can select a style of text (a headline, a bulleted list, a caption, or whatever) and type away. The style takes care of formatting the text for you. (You can also create character and page layout styles among other things, as you'll see in a moment.)

If you change the style later on, all the paragraphs in that style change automatically. So, for example, if you change a Heading style, all the headings in your document will change accordingly. In this way, using styles saves you the time and trouble of changing each heading individually.

Not My Style Don't panic—you don't have to create any styles if you don't want to. Each SmartMaster comes with a set of standard styles that you can use to format your text and easily change to fit your exact needs. Or if you don't want to deal with styles at all, you can forget them and modify each paragraph individually, as you learned how to do in Lesson 12. In addition, instead of creating character or page layout styles, you can change text or pages as you learned in Lessons 6 and 14.

If you don't select a style, Word Pro formats the text in the Default Text style, which is Times New Roman 12 point, left-aligned text. You can modify individual paragraphs manually, as you've learned how to do in previous lessons. Your modifications do not affect the style but rather the individual characteristics of a paragraph.

Assigning Styles to Text

When using styles, it helps to remember that Word Pro has already provided a set of standard styles for you—suited to the SmartMaster you choose when you began your new document. So if you chose a report-type SmartMaster, you already have the styles you would normally need for creating a report. For example, you'll probably find a Default Text style, a couple of bulleted and numbered list styles, and a few heading styles.

So before you type something into a document, you can just select an existing style from the Status bar, and what you type automatically conforms to the format of that style. You can also assign a style to existing text. Here's how to select a style:

1. If you've already typed some text, click inside the paragraph to which you want to assign a style. Otherwise, you can select a style before you type new text.

The More the Merrier You can assign a style to several paragraphs at once by selecting them first and then selecting a style.

2. Click on the Style Status button on the Status bar.

3. Select a paragraph style from the list (see Figure 15.1). Paragraph styles are marked with a backwards P. (Character styles are marked with an ABC icon, and Page layout styles are marked with a page icon. There are other styles too, as you'll learn in a minute.)

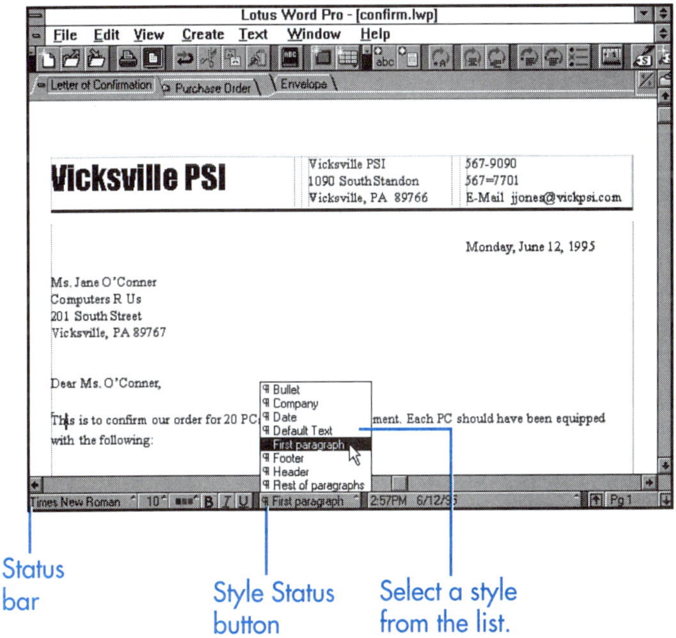

Figure 15.1 Select a style from the Status bar.

What Changes? Even if you've only highlighted one word or sentence in a paragraph, when you change the style for that paragraph, the *entire* paragraph changes to that style. However, slight alterations you may have made to the text in that paragraph (say, for instance, one word is italic, and another's in 8-point text) stay the same. This ensures that those small changes you make to your text aren't accidentally removed when you change paragraph styles.

You can also assign styles by using the F2 cycle key, or the Style Cycle button, located on the Text SmartIcon bar. When you press F2 or click on the Style Cycle button, your paragraph changes as it cycles through the list of available styles.

Undoing On-the-Spot Changes If you've made formatting changes to a paragraph (or other element) and you want to undo your additions, highlight the altered element, and then right-click. Select Named Styles from the pop-up menu, and then select Reset to Style. The highlighted element will go back to its original style. Manual changes that you've made to that element will disappear.

Other Kinds of Styles

So far we've talked about styles only in terms of paragraphs. But Word Pro supports other types of styles as well, such as *character styles*. A character style gives you a way to standardize text without affecting the way your paragraphs look. For example, you could create a character style called Tip and make it red, italic, 9 point text. Then you could insert tips *within* your paragraphs and make them stand out easily. Later, if you decide that all the tips should be 10 point text, you can change the style, and all the text in the Tip style will change accordingly.

Just about everything has a style assigned to it; for example, a table, a frame, and even a page has a standard style. As you'll see in just a minute, to create a style, you simply format a sample in the style you want, and then you give that style a name. For example, you could format a frame with a bold border and a 10 percent gray fill, call it Note, and use that frame style for all your notes within a document. (You'll learn how to create tables and frames in upcoming lessons.) You can also make changes to the standard style.

Once you create a style and save it, that style appears on the Style Status button on the Status bar. Character styles are marked with a small *abc* icon. Page styles appear with a small page icon, table styles appear with a small table icon, and so on.

Creating a Style

The easiest way to create a new style is to format a sample first, and then create a style from the example. For example, to create a paragraph style, format a paragraph (or a heading) the way you want, and then follow these steps to create and name a new paragraph style. See Lesson 12 for help in formatting a paragraph; see Lesson 6 for help in formatting characters (text); see upcoming lessons for help in formatting other elements such as tables, columns, and frames.

To create a new style from a sample, follow these steps:

1. Format a sample. For example, to create a paragraph style, format a paragraph the way you like.
2. Select your sample. To create a paragraph style, you don't have to select the entire thing. Just place the insertion point within the sample paragraph.
3. Click the right mouse button and select Named Styles from the pop-up menu.
4. Select Create. The Create Style dialog box appears, as shown in Figure 15.2.

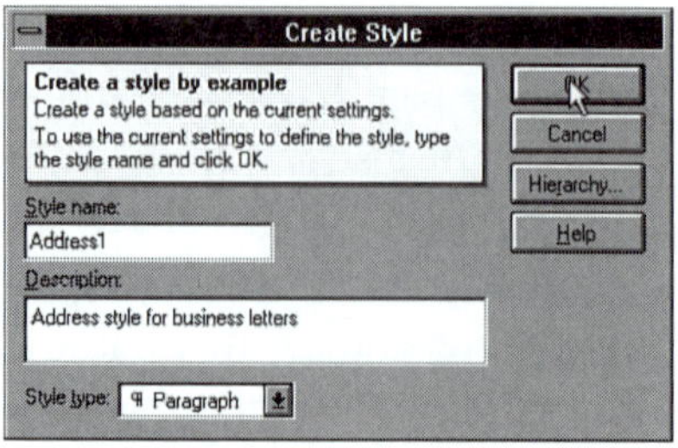

Figure 15.2 Giving a name to a new style.

5. Under Style name, type a name for your style.
6. Under Description, enter a brief description for this style, such as when (or on what) the style should be used.
7. Click on OK. Your new style is applied to the sample, and it appears on the Style Status button.

Fast Create You can also create a style by formatting a sample, opening the InfoBox, and clicking on the Style tab. Click on the Create Style button, type a name for your style, and click on OK. For example, to create a page layout style, right-click and select Page Properties to display the Page layout InfoBox. Then click on the Styles tab and click on Create Style.

Changing an Existing Style

From time to time, you'll want to change your style standards to suit new guidelines or just to modify the way your documents look. You might change the font or the margin settings for a paragraph and find yourself thinking, "Ah, this looks *better*." Word Pro lets you use those alterations to redefine the entire style; basically, you show Word Pro what you changed and tell it to make the same changes to the rest of the style.

To modify a style, follow these steps:

1. Select something in the style you want to change. For example, if you want to change the Heading style, select a heading.
2. Make the changes you want to save.
3. Select your sample. If you want to make changes to a paragraph style, you don't have to select it; instead, you can simply click inside the paragraph.
4. Click the right mouse button and select Named Styles from the pop-up menu, then select Redefine. The Redefine Style dialog appears, as shown in Figure 15.3.

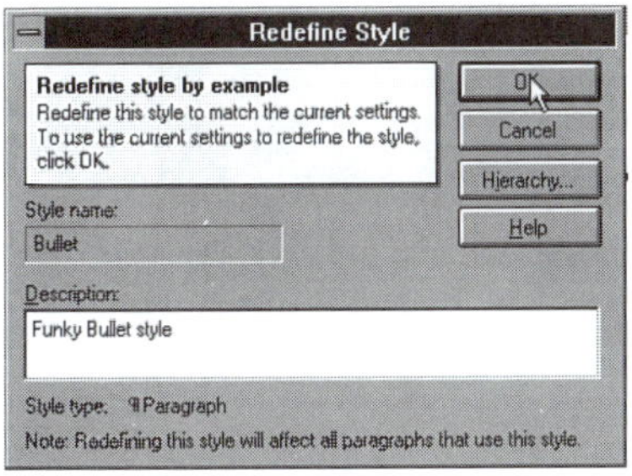

Figure 15.3 Redefining an existing style by example.

5. Click on OK. All elements formatted with that same style are altered to reflect the changes you made to the sample.

Redefining How To Change a Style You can also redefine a style from within the InfoBox. Just select the sample, click on the Style tab in the InfoBox, and then click on the Redefine Style button. Click on OK to redefine the style. For example, you could right-click, and select Text Properties to display the Text InfoBox. Then you could click on the Style tab and select the Heading style from the list and click on the Redefine Style button to change it.

Deleting or Renaming a Style

If for some reason you need to rename one of the styles in your document, or perhaps remove it entirely, follow these steps:

1. From within the InfoBox, click on the Style tab. To display an InfoBox, right-click and select the appropriate Properties command from the pop-up menu.
2. Click on the Manage Styles button. The Manage Styles dialog box appears (see Figure 15.4).

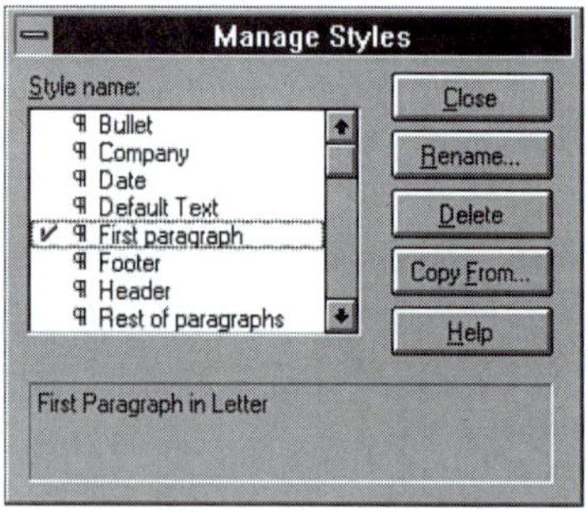

Figure 15.4 Advanced Style Management.

3. Select the style you want to change from the list. You can select several styles at one time if you're deleting them; if you're renaming them, you must select one at a time.
4. To delete the selected style(s), click on Delete and then click on Yes. To rename them, click on Rename and then enter a new name in the Rename Style dialog box. Then click on OK.
5. Click on Close.

In this lesson, you learned how to create and manage styles. You also learned how to assign styles to various elements, such as a paragraph, a frame, or a table. In the next lesson, you'll learn how to use the Ruler.

Lesson 16

Using the Ruler

In this lesson, you'll learn how to use the Ruler to set margins and indentations. You can also set tabs and the number of columns by using the Ruler; you'll learn how to do that in upcoming lessons.

Displaying the Ruler

There are two different Rulers in Word Pro: one that appears along the top of the document (and that's used to change the left and right margins, set indents, tabs, and column margins), and another that is located at the left side of the document (and that's used to change the top and bottom margins).

Rulers aren't placed in the middle of a page, unlike earlier versions of Word Pro (or Ami Pro, if you prefer). Instead, when you make changes to the page margins on the Ruler, it affects the entire document (unless you've divided your document into sections, in which case, it affects only the current section). If you make changes to the paragraph margins (indentation), your changes affect only the current paragraph. The current paragraph is the one in which the insertion point is located. To move the insertion point, simply click inside a different paragraph.

Please Make Your Selection Word Pro lets you make indentation changes to *selected paragraphs*, if you want. But regardless of how much of a paragraph you select, the entire paragraph will be reformatted based on the settings you select.

If you don't see a ruler as shown in Figure 16.1, take the following steps to make the Horizontal Ruler visible:

1. Open the View menu and select Show/Hide.
2. Select Ruler. The Horizontal Ruler appears at the top of the document window, as shown in Figure 16.1.

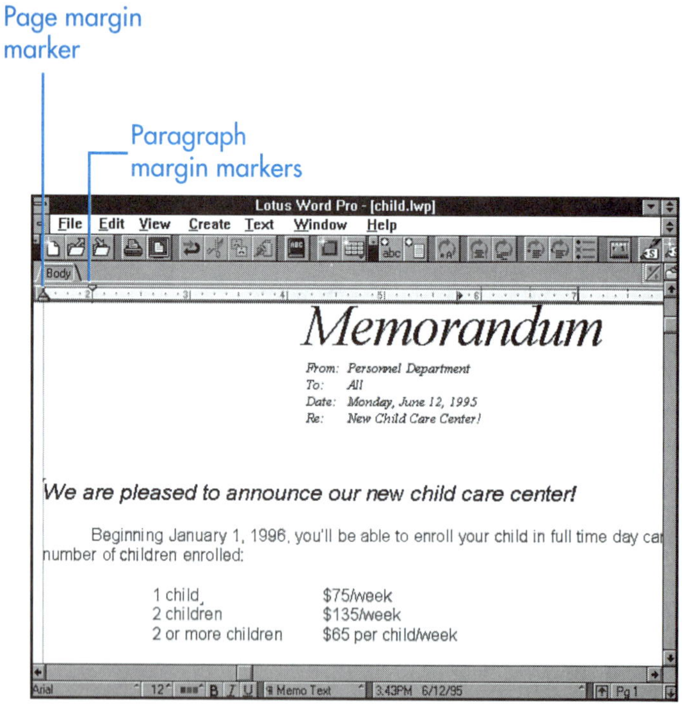

Figure 16.1 The Horizontal Ruler is the most often used.

The Horizontal Ruler in Word Pro is reminiscent of the margin/tab controls on a standard typewriter. The yellow area in the middle represents the region of the page where you may currently type text. On both sides of this yellow area are gray rectangular bars, which represent the margins of the *page*. If you move one or both of these bars, you change the left and/or right page margins, as you'll see soon.

Just inside these gray bars are half-diamond shaped notches, which represent the margins of the *paragraph*. If you move one of these, you change the margins (or more properly, the *indentation*) of selected paragraphs.

Since it's only used to set the top and bottom margins, you might not need the Vertical Ruler as often as the Horizontal Ruler; for that reason, the Vertical Ruler isn't displayed when you select Show/Hide Ruler. To display it, follow these steps:

1. Open the View menu and select Set View Preferences. The View Preferences dialog appears, as shown in Figure 16.2.

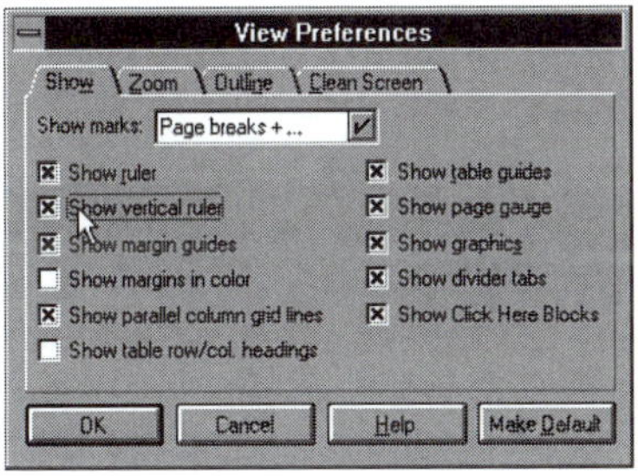

Figure 16.2 Deciding what gets seen and what doesn't.

2. Click on the Show tab.
3. Select the Show vertical ruler check box.
4. Click on OK to close the dialog box.

Setting Margins with the Ruler

The Ruler has many special marks that are used in setting margins, as shown in Figure 16.3.

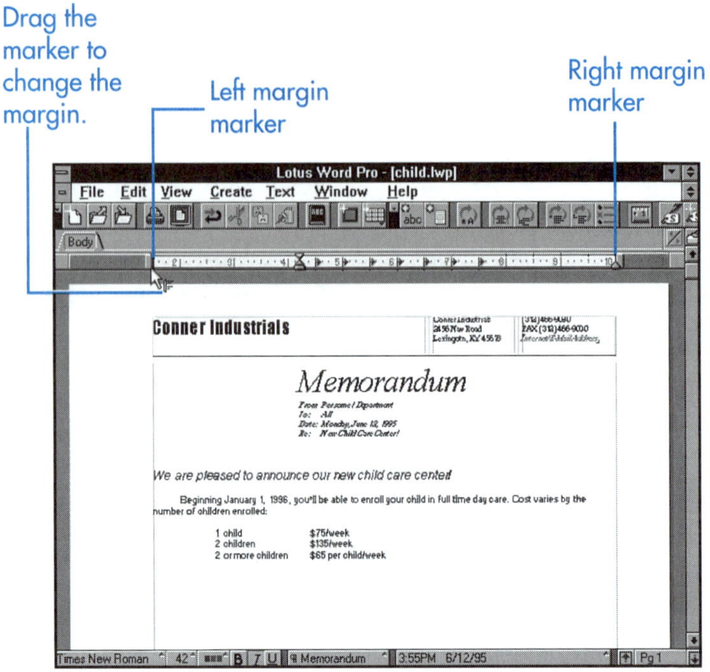

Figure 16.3 The special gray boxes for setting margins are located on the Ruler.

To change the margins of a page with the Ruler, follow these steps:

1. Display the Horizontal Ruler.
2. To set the left or right margin, click on the appropriate marker.
3. Drag the pointer to the desired location. As you drag, you'll see a shadow margin line on your document, which shows you relatively where the new margin will be.
4. Release the mouse button, and the margin is reset.

Notice that when you let go of the mouse button, the yellow area inside the Ruler expands or contracts to fit the new text area. Also notice that when you reset the *left page* margin, the *left paragraph* margins scoot with the page margin; they don't stay where you originally put them.

> **What Pages Does This Affect?** Your margin change affects the current section of the document, regardless of which page you're on. If you want to affect selected pages within a section (such as all the left-hand pages), use the Page Layout InfoBox, as described in Lesson 14. To change margins from a particular point in the document, insert a new page layout, and then change the margins as you like (see Lesson 14). You can also create a new division or section (see Lesson 19).

To change the top or bottom margins of your document, display the Vertical Ruler and drag the corresponding marker. Moving the upper margin down gives more room for the page header. When you place the insertion point in the page header region, the Vertical Ruler changes to show you the margins for the header region. The same holds true for the footer region at the bottom of pages. (You'll learn more about headers and footers in Lesson 18.)

Setting Indentations with the Ruler

The Ruler has a handful of special markers that are used in setting paragraph margins and indentations, as shown in Figure 16.4.

There are two markers that control the left margin or indent. The top marker affects only the first line of a paragraph, while the bottom marker affects all the lines *but the first one*. To indent the entire paragraph, you move both of these markers together, as you'll see in a moment.

The right margin marker affects all the lines in a paragraph. Again, remember that the changes you make affect only the current (or selected) paragraph(s).

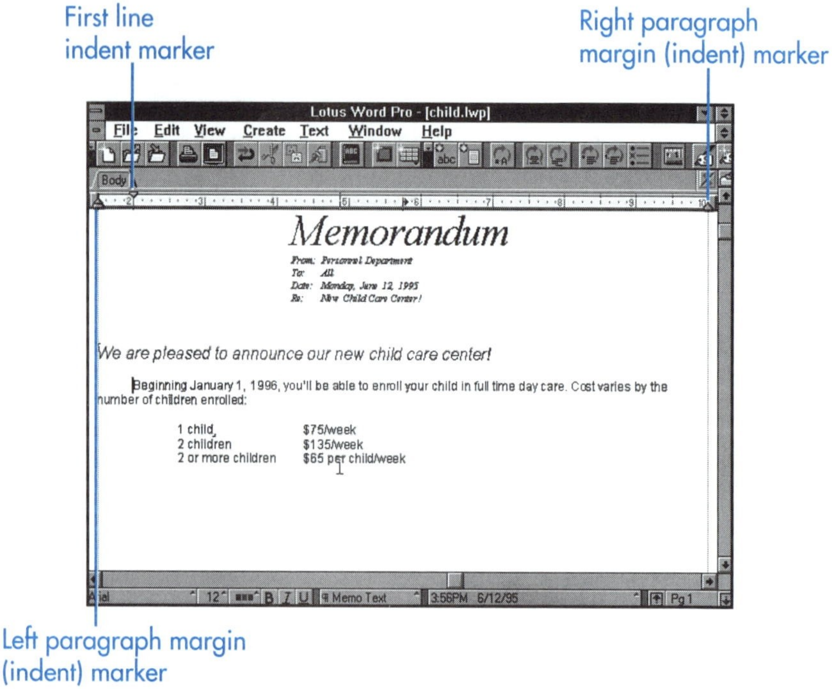

Figure 16.4 The special marks for setting indentations are located on the Ruler.

To change the margins (indentations) of a paragraph with the Ruler, follow these steps:

1. Display the Horizontal Ruler.
2. Place the insertion point within the paragraph whose settings you intend to change. To change multiple paragraphs at once, select them now.
3. Drag the appropriate marker:

- To set the indentation of just the first line in a paragraph, click on the upper line indentation triangle and drag it to the desired location.
- To set the indentation of the rest of the lines in a paragraph (besides the first line), click on the lower line indentation triangle and drag it to the desired location.
- To change *all* the settings for the left paragraph margin, click and hold the rectangular bar on the *bottom* of the Ruler, drag this bar to a new position, and release the mouse button.
- To change the right margin indent, click on the right paragraph indent marker and drag it to the desired location.

Where's the Margin Release? Page margins in Word Pro are just guidelines. You can set the margins for a paragraph *outside* of the page margin boundaries if you want, and Word Pro will accept those settings. Using outdented headings can be quite effective in a report.

In this lesson, you learned how to use the Ruler to change the indentations (or margins) for selected paragraphs. You also learned how to use the Ruler to change the margins for a page. In the next lesson, you'll learn how to set tabs.

Lesson 17

Setting Tabs

In this lesson, you'll learn how to set tabs with the Ruler.

Understanding the Different Tab Types

Tabs in Word Pro, like tabs on a typewriter, are points that the cursor jumps to when you press Tab. Unlike a typewriter, however, text can be made to "lean" against a tab stop in a particular way. Here are examples of the various tab types:

Left Aligns characters to the left of the tab. For example, a left tab aligns the first letters in this list of names:

Jane
Scott
Mary Beth

Right Aligns characters to the right of the tab. For example, a right tab aligns the colons in this list of headings:

Description:
Syntax:
Example:

Numeric Used when aligning numbers at a decimal point. For example, a numeric tab aligns these numbers at their decimal points:

$121.32
.05
–29.0767

Center Centers the text around the tab. For example, a center tab centers each of these lines on a single point:

This is an example
of centered tabs
The tab is located above
the n in the first line.

As an option, you can precede your tabbed characters with a *leader*. You can choose from several different leaders: Underline, Dash, Period, and None. For example, you could use a period as a leader:

Chapter .... Page

Introduction 1
Chapter 5
Chapter 11

Leader A leader is a character that fills the spaces between items in a tabbed list.

Setting a Tab

Left tabs are already set for you, at 1/2-inch intervals. You can change these tab settings or add your own with the Ruler. By default, the tabs you set by clicking on the Ruler are Left tabs, but you can set other tab types, as well.

Tabs are set only for the current paragraph, unless you select several paragraphs first. In either case, setting tabs is easy with the Ruler:

1. If the Ruler is not displayed, click on the Show/Hide Ruler button, or open the View menu and select Show/Hide, then select Ruler.
2. To remove all preset tabs first, right-click on the Ruler and select Clear All Tabs from the menu that appears.
3. If you want to, right-click on the Ruler and change the tab type by clicking on Create Left Tabs, Create Right Tabs, Create Centered Tabs, or Create Numeric Tabs.
4. Click on the point on the ruler where you want the tab to appear. A tab mark appears at that point (see Figure 17.1).

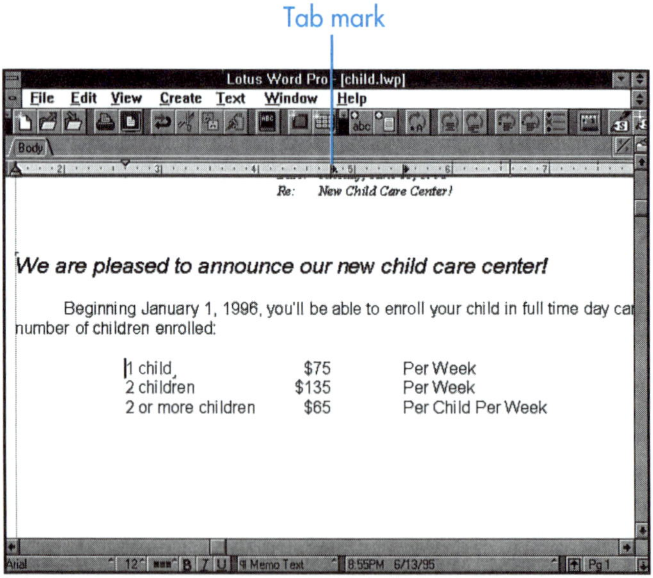

Figure 17.1 The tab setting buttons are located on the Ruler.

If you want to set a tab in the exact center of your page, or a tab at the exact right-hand margin, then right-click on the Ruler and select either Quick Center Tab or Quick Right Tab.

Put It on My Tab To move an existing tab, simply drag the tab mark to its new location. To *remove* a tab, drag it off the Ruler entirely. You can drag a tab mark above or below the ruler area to remove it.

Using a Dialog Box to Set Tabs

If you want to be more precise about setting tabs, you can set and move tabs by typing their location into the Set Tabs on Ruler dialog box. You can also use this dialog box to select a tab leader. Here's how it works:

1. Right-click on the Ruler and select Set Tabs. The Set Tabs on Ruler dialog box appears, as shown here:

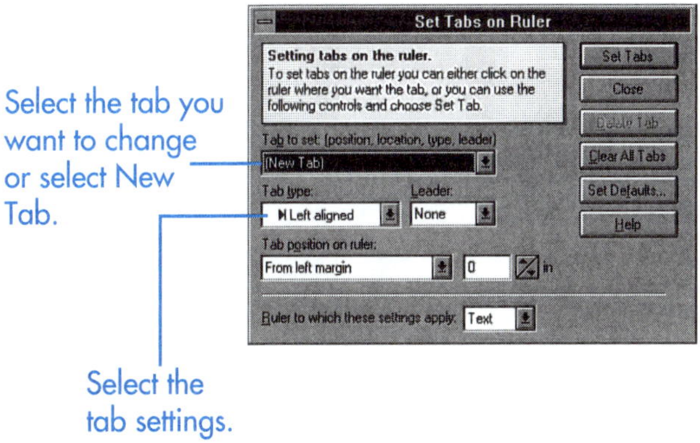

Figure 17.2 Use this dialog box for precise tab adjustments.

2. To change an existing tab, select it from the Tab to set list. Otherwise, select (New Tab) from the list.
3. Choose the type of tab you want to set from the Tab type list.
4. To precede the tab with a leader character, select one from the Leader list.
5. The position of a tab is generally based on its location relative to one of the margins. Select which margin to use from the Tab position on ruler list.
6. Set the distance from the chosen margin by entering an amount in inches in the corresponding text box.
7. To set your tab, click on Set Tabs.
8. Repeat steps 2 through 7 to set additional tabs. When you're done, click on Close.

In this lesson, you learned how to set various types of tabs. In the next lesson, you'll learn how to create headers and footers.

Lesson 18

Creating Headers and Footers

In this lesson, you'll learn how to create headers and footers for your Word Pro document.

What Are Headers and Footers?

A *header* is a collection of characters, such as a report title, which appears at the top of each page of a document (unless otherwise specified). A *footer* is similar to a header except that it appears at the bottom of every page (unless otherwise specified).

Headers and footers are "built-into" every document by default—but they're blank. That means they're there, but they won't actually print until you add text, page numbers, and graphics to them (see Figure 18.1).

So Where's the Header or Footer? If you can't see your header or footer, open the View menu and select Show/Hide. Then select Headers & Footers.

If you change a header or footer, Word Pro changes the header or footer throughout that section of the document regardless of which page you make your changes on. You can create a different header or footer at a specific point in the document by inserting a page layout (see Lesson 14) or by adding sections (see Lesson 19).

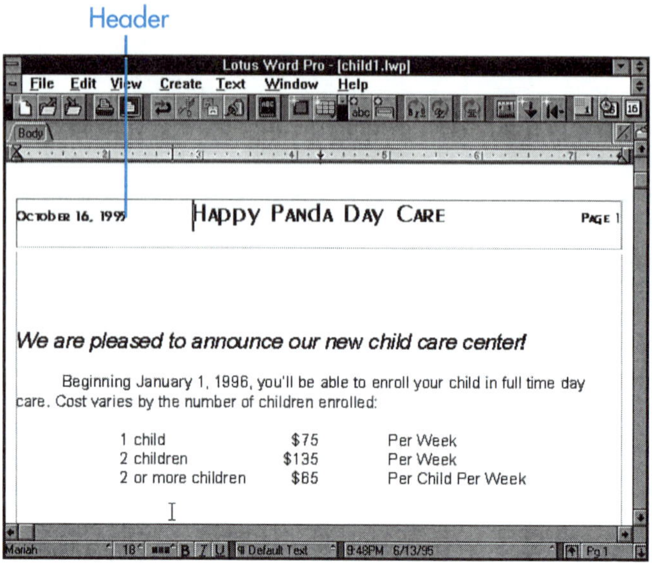

Figure 18.1 A sample header.

You can also use the new page layout to create a header or footer for the left pages of a document that is different from the one that appears on the right. For example, this book displays the lesson number on the left page, and the lesson title on the right.

Creating a Header or Footer

Again, although a header and a footer already exist within a document, they are empty. Follow these steps to add text, page numbers, or graphics to your header or footer to "create" them:

1. Click inside the header or footer area. (If you can't see the header or footer area, open the View menu and select Show/Hide. Then select Headers & Footers.)
2. Type the text for the header or footer. You can select a different font and other attributes (such as bold, italics, centered alignment, and so on) for your text as needed.

Center Stage To center something in your header or footer, insert a center tab by right-clicking on the Ruler and selecting Quick Center Tab. Then press Tab and insert your text. You can right-align something by selecting Quick Right Tab instead.

3. To add a date or the time, right-click and select Date/Time from the menu that appears to display the Insert Date/Time dialog box. You learned about this dialog box (see Figure 18.2) in Lesson 4. Click on the Date or Time option, and select the style you like from the list. Then click on OK.

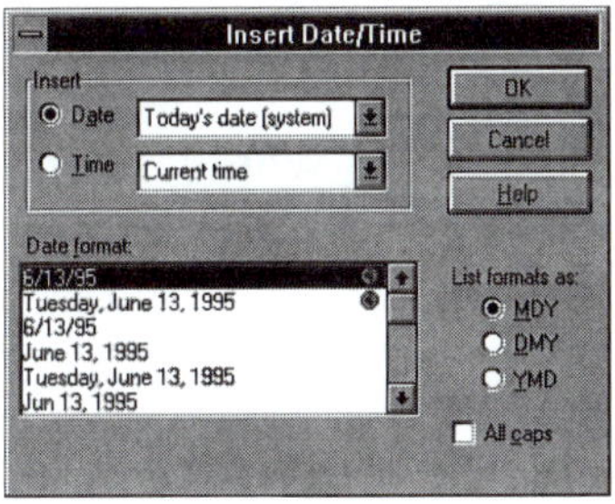

Figure 18.2 Adding a date to the header.

4. To add a page number, right-click and select Insert Page Number from the menu that appears to display the Insert Page Number dialog box. This is the same dialog box (see Figure 18.3) you learned how to use in Lesson 14. Select the page number type you want to use from the Number list and change other settings as needed. Click on OK.

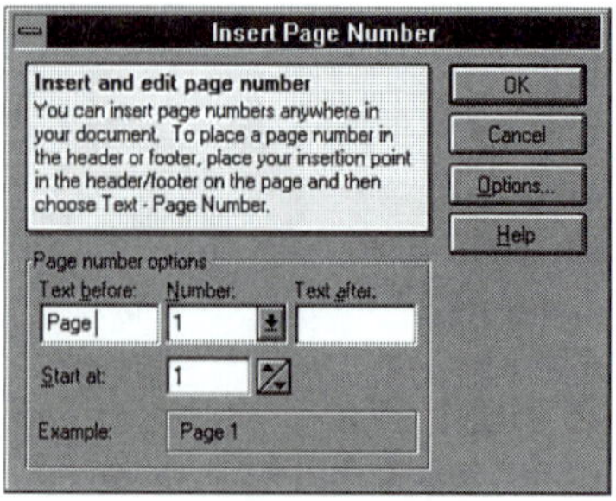

Figure 18.3 Adding a page number.

5. When you are done, click within the document.

Changing Other Header or Footer Properties

Like most every other object in Word Pro, headers and footers have their own sets of properties. You can set header and footer margins, add lines, colors, or shadows, and set other properties with an InfoBox.

To open the InfoBox, follow these steps:

1. Right-click on the header or footer.
2. Select Header Properties or Footer Properties from the pop-up menu that appears. The Header or Footer InfoBox appears, as shown in Figure 18.4.

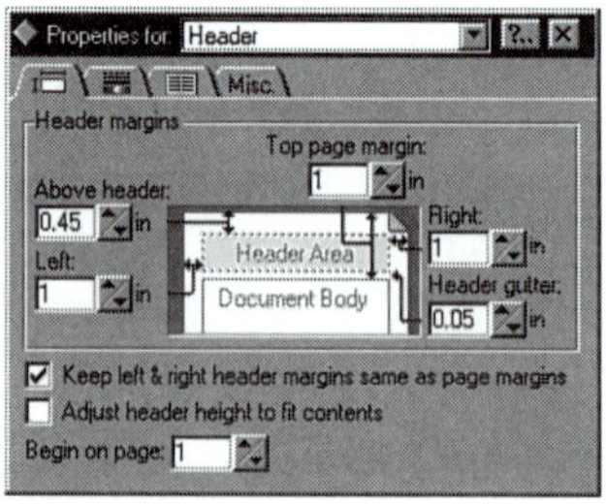

Figure 18.4 Fine-tune your header or footer with the InfoBox.

With the InfoBox, you can set the margins for your header or footer by number rather than by estimate, as you would with the Ruler. Notice that there's a setting here that you don't find on the Ruler marked *gutter*. This is the amount of space between the header and the top edge of your body text. There's a similar gutter between the lower edge of body text and the footer area.

Where Else Can I Find My Properties? Header and footer properties are also located in the Page Layout InfoBox on the Header or Footer tab.

In this lesson, you learned how to create headers and footers. In addition, you learned how to insert a date, time, or page number into a header or footer. In the next lesson, you'll learn how to make formal divisions in your document.

Lesson 19

Using Divisions and Sections to Manage a Long Document

In this lesson, you'll learn how to break Word Pro documents into divisions and sections.

Sections and Divisions: What's the Difference?

In Word Pro, you have the capability to divide a document into divisions or sections. Among other things, this allows you to easily reorganize a long document, or select a unique style for part of a document. When determining whether or not to use a division or a section to organize a document, keep these things in mind:

- A division is treated like a new document.
- Divisions always start on a new page.
- A division is not created from text that's already in the document; instead, it is inserted into a document at the selected point.
- A division can use a different SmartMaster from the main document.
- A division can be a file imported from another program, such as Lotus 1-2-3.

A section, meanwhile, doesn't constitute as deep a separation as a division. That's because a section can be any amount of text, even just a paragraph. The following points apply to sections:

- Sections don't have to start on a new page.
- Sections use the same SmartMaster as the main document, but they can have their own page layout. (This means that sections can have their own headers, footers, page numbering system, and so on.)
- Sections allow you to use different page layouts on the same page.

Regardless of whether you use divisions or sections (or both), you can use the resulting tabs (which appear at the top of a document window) to reorganize a document quickly and easily. You'll learn how to do this in a moment; first, let's learn how to create divisions and sections.

Creating a Division

As mentioned earlier, divisions act like separate documents. By definition, a division has its own SmartMaster associated with it. For example, you might import a newsletter page formatted with one SmartMaster into a report formatted with another.

To create a division, follow these steps:

1. Place the insertion point where you want the division to begin. (Remember that a division must start on a new page, so a page break will occur at the spot you select.)
2. Open the Create menu and select Division. The Create Division dialog box appears (see Figure 19.1).

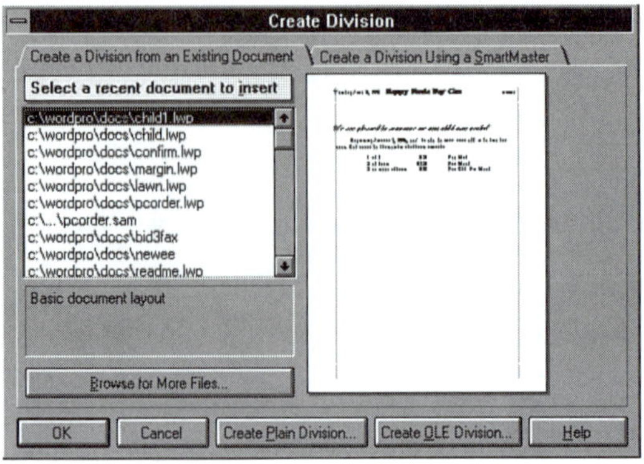

Figure 19.1 Creating a division.

3. Select how you want to create your division:

   - To create a division with an existing Word Pro document, click on the Create a Division from an Existing Document tab and select your document from the list. You can click on the Browse for More Files button and search for a file if you want to.
   - To create a new division based on an existing SmartMaster, click on the Create a Division Using a SmartMaster tab, then choose a SmartMaster from the list.
   - To simply create a division without applying styles to it, click on the Create Plain Division button.

The Insert Division dialog box appears, shown in Figure 19.2.

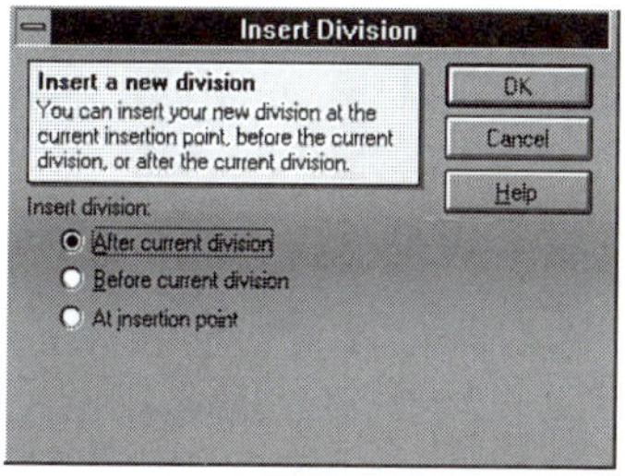

Figure 19.2 The act of inserting a division.

4. Select the appropriate option button to insert the new division either after the current division, before the current division, or at the insertion point.

5. Choose how you want the new division saved: as part of the document file or only linked to it.

6. Click on OK. The division is inserted.

The End, or a New Beginning? Your new division begins with a new page. This may mean the creation of white space at the end of the prior division.

Creating a Section

A section is a portion of a document that can have its own independent page formatting. Unlike a division, a section is always formatted using the same SmartMaster as the document or division to which it belongs. Also unlike a division, a section can be created by dividing the existing text within a document.

To create a new section, follow these steps:

1. Place the insertion point where you want the new section to begin.

2. Open the Create menu and select Section. The Create Section dialog appears, as shown in Figure 19.3.

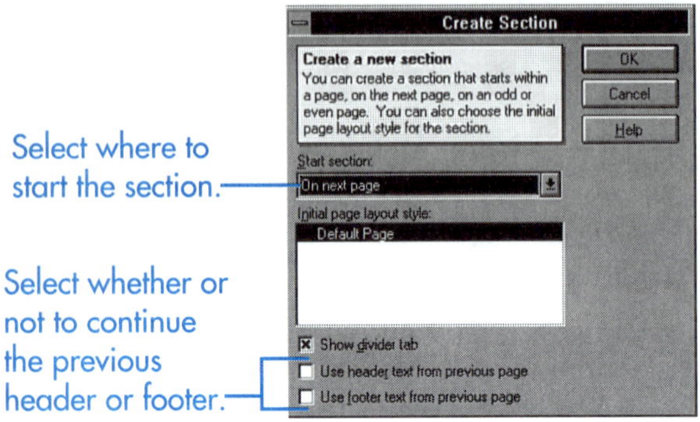

Figure 19.3 The Create Section dialog box.

3. Select where to begin the new section from the Start section list.

4. In the Initial page layout style list are page styles associated with the current document or division. To change page styles, choose one from this list.

5. If you don't want Word Pro to create a tab for your new section, click on the Show divider tab option to deselect it.

6. To continue the header or footer text from the previous section, select Use header text from previous page and/or Use footer text from previous page.

7. Click on OK. The new section is created.

What's This? Word Pro marks the beginning of a section with a small file-folder icon. But don't worry; it doesn't print—you see it only in the document window.

Using Divider Tabs

When you start most documents, they contain one tab, marked "Body." After you create a division or a section, a new tab appears at the top of the document window. These tabs give you instant access to the document's various divisions and sections, as shown in Figure 19.4.

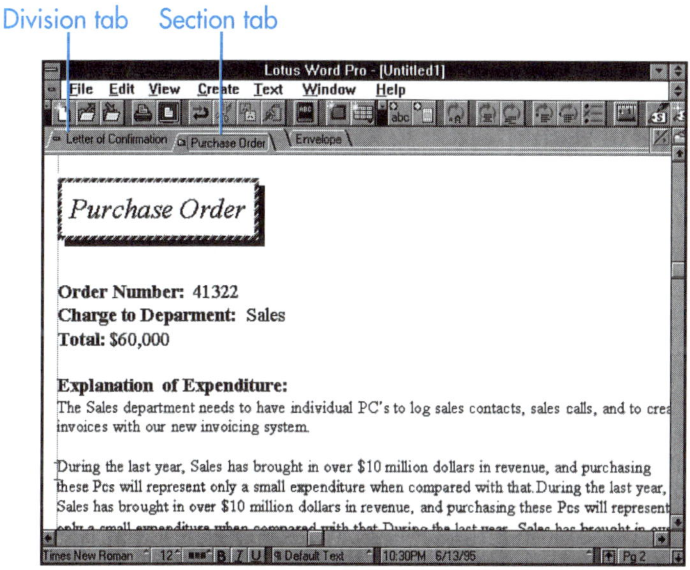

Figure 19.4 An easy way to thumb through Word Pro.

Don't See the Tabs! If you don't see the tabs, look for a file folder button along the right side of the document window. Click on this button to display the tabs.

The tabs may look similar, but if you look closely, you'll notice that a section tab is marked with a file folder icon, while a division tab that contains a section is marked with a minus sign.

Here are some things you can do with tabs:

- To move to a particular section or division, click on the appropriate tab.
- You can tell what the current tab is because it appears "indented."
- You can rename a tab by double-clicking on it and then typing a name.
- To reorganize a document using the tabs, you can click on the tab you want to move and drag it to its new location.

You can even change the color of a tab. Here's how:

1. Right-click on the tab and select Division Properties or Section Properties from the menu that appears to display a dialog box. The Division Properties dialog box is shown in Figure 19.5.

Select a color for your tab.

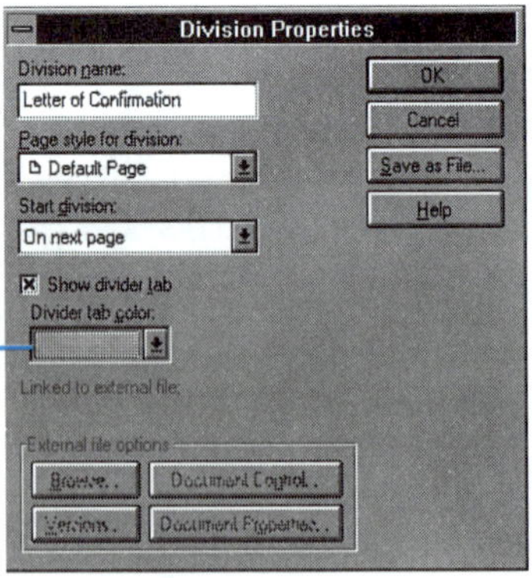

Figure 19.5 Colorizing a tab.

2. Select a color from the Divider tab color list.
3. Click on OK.

In this lesson, you learned how to manage large Word Pro documents by creating divisions and sections. In the next lesson, you'll learn how to customize SmartIcons.

Lesson 20

Customizing SmartIcons

In this lesson, you'll learn how to customize the Word Pro SmartIcons.

Hiding and Displaying SmartIcons

SmartIcons are grouped based on function in iconbars. When you first start Word Pro, the Universal and the Text SmartIcon bars are visible. As you work, other SmartIcon bars automatically appear to help you. However, you can remove these iconbars if you prefer to work with a clearer screen. Here's how to remove all the iconbars:

1. Open the View menu and select Show/Hide.
2. Select SmartIcons.

To redisplay the hidden SmartIcons, just open the View menu, select Show/Hide, and then select SmartIcons again. To remove a particular SmartIcon bar (instead of all of them), follow these steps:

1. Click once on the iconbar's bar button (see Figure 20.1).
2. Select Hide this SmartIcon bar from the pop-up menu. The iconbar disappears.

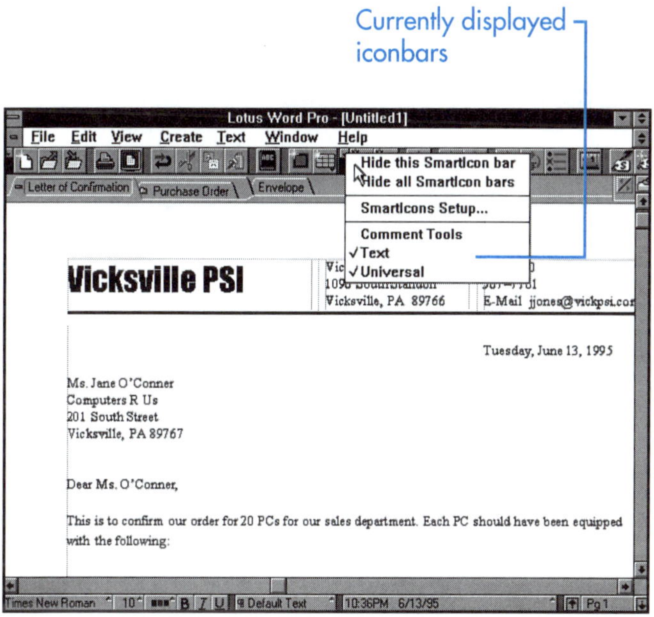

Figure 20.1 Hiding a single iconbar is easy.

A hidden IconBar is still "active," which means it's fairly easy to redisplay it. Here's how:

1. Click once on the bar button of *some other* iconbar.
2. Select the iconbar you want to redisplay from the list.

Moving the SmartIcon IconBar

SmartIcons normally appear at the top of the document window. Although just below the menu bar may be the most convenient place for Word Pro, you may find that you'd like to move them elsewhere—perhaps along another edge of the window or floating someplace in the work area. Figure 20.2 shows some of the other locations that SmartIcon palettes may be located.

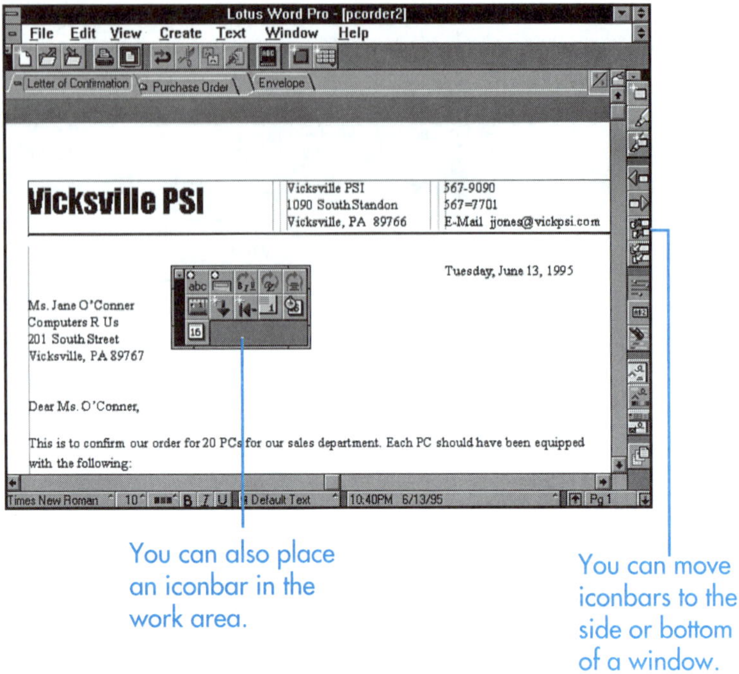

Figure 20.2 SmartIcons everywhere you look.

To move a SmartIcon palette to another location, follow these steps:

1. Move the pointer over the iconbar's bar button (a small vertical rectangle that is the same color as a window's title bar). A hand icon appears.

2. Click and hold onto the bar button.

3. Drag the iconbar to its new location and release the mouse button. You can move the iconbar to any window edge or into the middle of the work area.

When you move an iconbar into the work area, Word Pro puts a stretchable frame around it. Just click on a frame edge and drag to reshape the palette, as shown in Figure 20.2.

Customizing the SmartIcon IconBar

After working with SmartIcons for awhile, you may want to customize them more to your liking. You can easily add and/or remove SmartIcons from any iconbar. Here's how you do it:

1. Open the File menu and select User Setup.
2. Select SmartIcons Setup. The SmartIcons Setup dialog box appears, as shown in Figure 20.3.

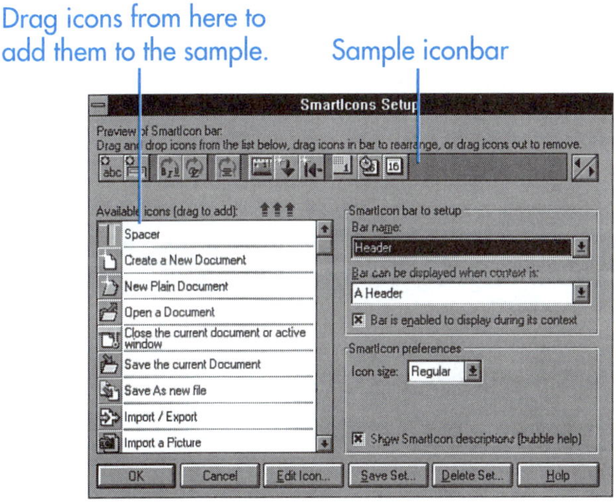

Figure 20.3 Customizing an iconbar.

3. Select the iconbar you want to customize from the Bar name list. A sample of your iconbar appears at the top of the dialog box.
4. To add a SmartIcon, drag it from the Available icons list onto the sample iconbar. To remove a SmartIcon, drag it off the sample iconbar.
5. To group a set of icons together, add a space by dragging the Spacer onto the sample iconbar.

6. To display SmartIcons in another size, select it from the Icon size list.

7. Word Pro displays an iconbar when you select an object of a particular type. To change when the sample iconbar automatically appears, select a different object from the Bar can be displayed when context is list.

8. If you don't want the SmartIcon bar to autmatically display when you select a particular object, but you want to be able to display it by selecting from the pop-up menu, then deselect the Bar is enabled to display during its context option.

9. To disable bubble help, click on the Show SmartIcon descriptions (bubble help) option to deselect it.

10. To create a new iconbar, make your selections and then click on Save Set. Give your new set a name, and then click on OK.

11. When you're through, click on OK.

In this lesson, you learned how to customize SmartIcon iconbars, as well as how to create new ones. In the next lesson, you'll learn how to create a frame.

Lesson 21

Creating Frames

This is the first of two lessons on the subject of frames. In this lesson, you'll learn how to create text frames and graphic frames.

What Are Frames?

If you were to study the layout of a newspaper or a magazine, you would find rectangular areas around which the text flows. These rectangles contain photographs with captions, quotes pulled from the article you're reading, graphics, advertisements, and other items. These rectangles are considered *frames.*

In Word Pro, you can create frames and place them wherever you want on a page. Text that you type into a frame stays within that rectangular area. If you move a frame, that text travels with the frame to its new location. This is the same for anything else you might put in a frame, such as a graphic, a table, or even another frame. In designing a newsletter or a report, you almost certainly will be using columns (covered in Lesson 23) and frames.

You can resize a frame and change its border. You can also fill a frame with color. In addition, you can layer part of a frame on top of another. Figure 21.1 shows various types of frames you can create in Word Pro.

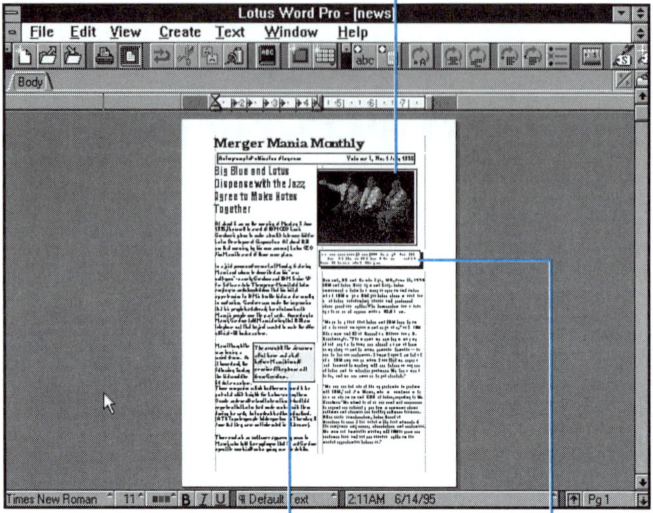

Figure 21.1 A text and graphics frame in its most common surroundings.

Creating a Text Frame

In Word Pro, text in a frame is independent from the body of the document. This means you can move the text frame anywhere you want on the page. A text frame can contain more than just text; it can contain a table, columns, and even another frame.

You create a text frame by drawing the frame *first*, and then filling it with text (or whatever). Here's how you draw the frame:

1. Click on the Create Frame button on the Universal SmartIcon bar.

2. Click in the document to establish the upper left corner of the frame.

3. Drag downward and to the right to create the frame, as shown in Figure 21.2.

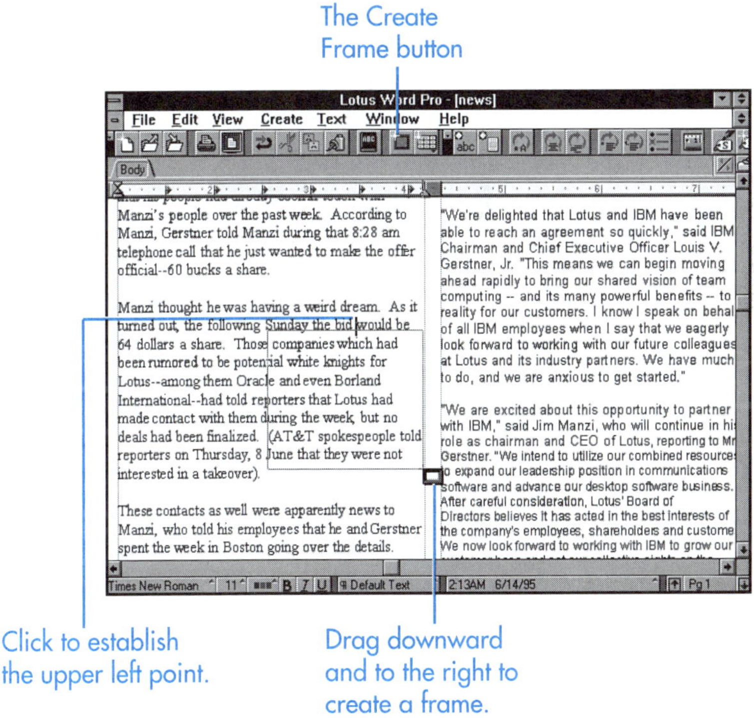

Figure 21.2 Drawing a frame.

Wrong Size! To create a frame with a precise width and height, you can use the Create Frame dialog box. Just open the Create menu and select Frame. Then enter the dimensions you want and click on OK.

Typing Text into a Frame

Immediately after you create a frame, the blinking cursor appears inside it so you can start typing text. Formatting and styling text works the same way here as it does anywhere else in Word Pro; you choose fonts, point sizes, and other attributes, as you learned in Lesson 6. You can also format text using a style, as discussed in Lesson 15. So the rules of text here are pretty much the same as anywhere else (see Figure 21.3).

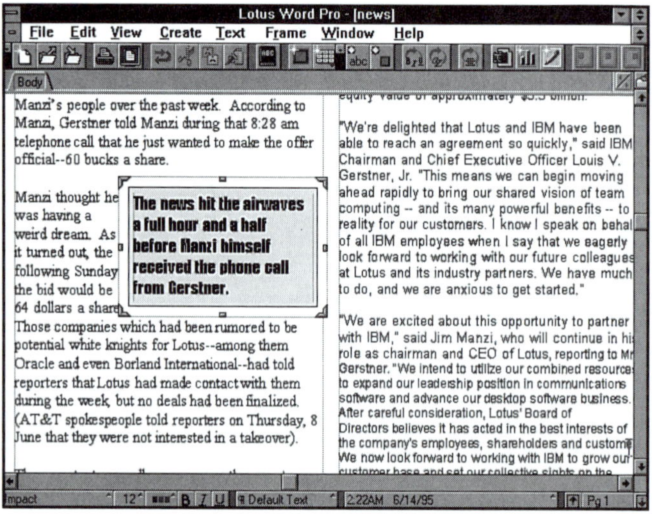

Figure 21.3 Word Pro automatically wraps your text within the frame.

Notice that when you type in a frame, Word Pro wraps your words automatically within the frame borders. When you're through typing text, click outside the frame.

Space Unavailable? If you're typing text into a frame and suddenly your cursor disappears, and you can't see what you're typing anymore, your text is *not lost*. Instead, it's simply being held in a special place until you resize the frame. When you make the frame bigger, your text will reappear. You'll learn how to resize a frame in the next lesson.

Creating a Graphic Frame

When you import a graphic (picture) from another source into Word Pro, that picture is automatically placed within a frame of its own. You don't need to create a frame and then import the graphic. Once the graphic has been imported, you can reposition and resize the frame as necessary, just as you would a text frame.

To import a graphic into a document, follow these steps:

1. Place the insertion point where you want the *upper left corner* of the graphic to appear.

2. Open the File menu and select Import Picture. The Import Picture dialog box appears, as shown in Figure 21.4.

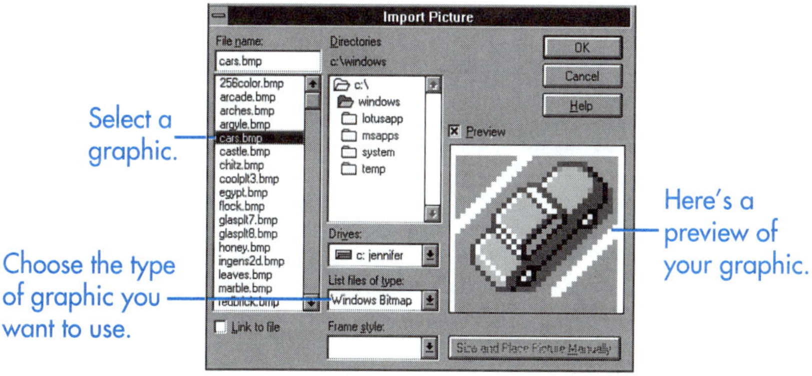

Figure 21.4 A link to all your pictures and clip art.

3. Select the type of graphic you want to import from the List files of type list.

4. Change to the drive and directory in which the graphic you want to use is stored.

5. Select the graphic from the File name list. A preview of the graphic appears.

6. If you want, select a frame style from the Frame style list.

7. Click on OK. Word Pro places your graphic at the insertion point.

If you want to add a caption to your figure and keep the two elements together, create a large text frame for the caption and insert the graphic frame into the text frame. (Remember, you can put anything in a frame, including another frame—just click inside the first frame and follow these steps to insert a graphic frame into it.)

Adjusting Your Graphic Image

Once you import your graphic, you can adjust some of its characteristics so that it will look and print better. Double-click on the image to select it. Then right-click, and select Image Properties from the menu that appears. (If you don't see the Image Properties command, then your graphic cannot be adjusted in this manner.)

The Image Properties dialog box, shown in Figure 21.5, contains dials for adjusting the brightness, hue, and contrast of the graphic image. You can play with these settings and click on Apply to try them out. Once you find a suitable adjustment, click on OK; or click on Cancel to revert to the image as it was.

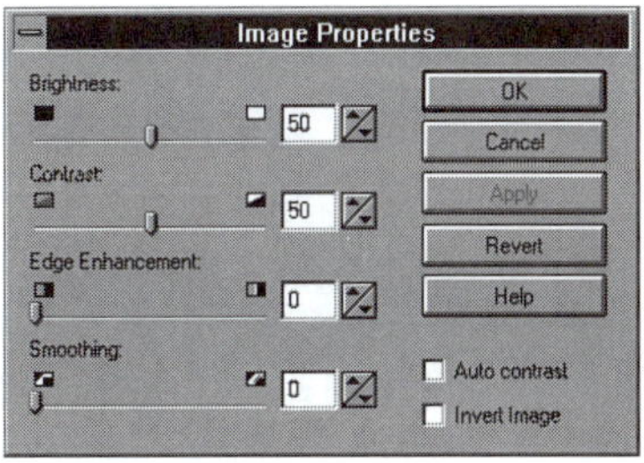

Figure 21.5 The "remote control" for graphics properties.

In this lesson, you learned how to create text and graphic frames. In the next lesson, you'll learn more about frames, including how to resize, move, and delete a frame.

Lesson 22

Working with Frames

In this lesson, you'll learn how to resize, move, copy, and delete a frame, how to anchor a frame to some text, and how to change the way the frame appears.

Selecting a Frame

To work with a frame, you must select it. When you do, the frame's border changes to show you that it's selected. Once selected, you can change the frame's properties and copy, move, or delete it. But there's an important difference between selecting a frame and selecting its contents. If you want to change the contents of a frame (such as the text it contains), then you must select the frame's contents and not the frame itself.

> **Handle** A *handle* is a marker that appears along the edge of an object when it is selected. A frame is considered an *object* because it is independent from the document as a whole. Handles are used to "grab" an object for selection and resizing.
>
> Plain English

To select a frame's contents or the frame itself, do the following:

1. Click once within the area of the frame. Word Pro surrounds the frame with frame handles along the sides and at the corners (see Figure 22.1). At this point, you have selected the frame's inner contents, so the cursor appears inside.

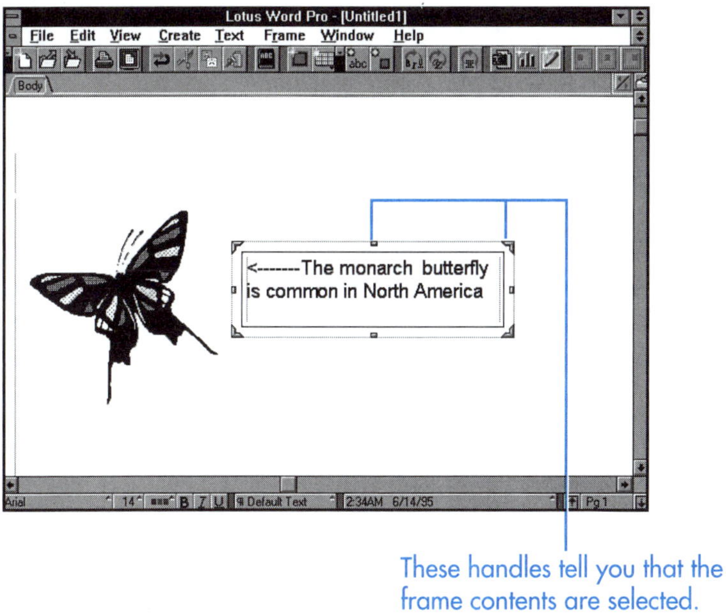

Figure 22.1 A frame whose contents have been selected.

2. Move the pointer toward the outer perimeter. The pointer assumes the shape of an open hand.

3. Click once on this outer perimeter. The frame appears solid (see Figure 22.2). At this point, you have selected the frame, not what it contains. You are now free to fully manipulate the frame.

For a *graphics frame* (a frame with only graphics in it and no text), the selection process is a bit different. To select a graphics frame, just click once. The frame itself is now selected. As you'll see later in the lesson, to select the contents of a graphics frame, you double-click on it.

Notice that there are two types of handles: *resizing handles* and *relocator handles*. Resizing handles are located at each corner and in the center of all four sides of the outer perimeter. Relocator handles, which are used to move the frame, are in between the resizing handles.

Is It a Resizer or a Relocator? To know for sure whether you're pointing to a resizing handle or a relocator handle, just look at the pointer. If the pointer is in the shape of a *hand*, you're pointing to a relocator handle. If the pointer is in the shape of a *two-pointer arrow*, you're pointing to a resizing handle.

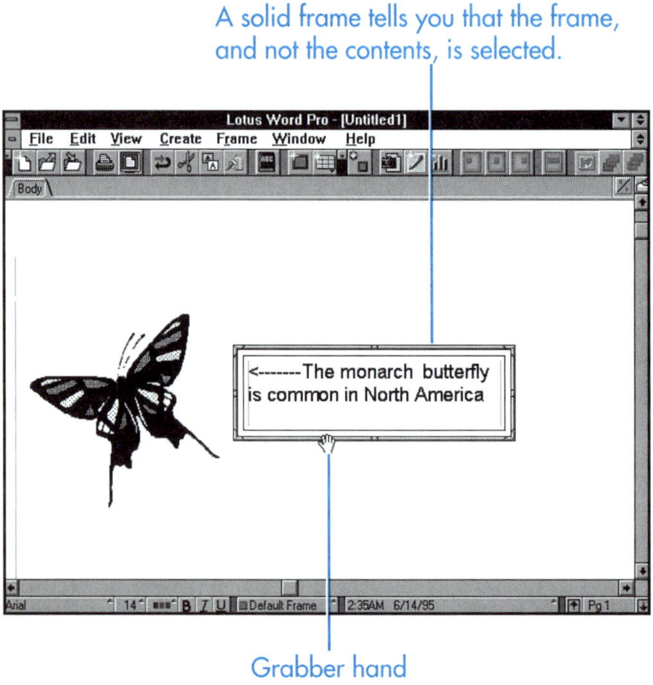

Figure 22.2 A frame that has been selected.

Copying, Moving, and Deleting Frames

You can easily copy, move, and delete frames as necessary. When you copy a frame, you copy its contents, as well.

To copy, move, or delete a frame, you have to select the frame itself. A frame is selected when it is surrounded by a solid frame (see the previous section for help in selecting frames).

To copy a frame, follow these steps:

1. Select the frame to copy.
2. Click on the Copy SmartIcon.
3. Click in the location within the document to which you want to copy the frame.
4. Click on the Paste SmartIcon. A copy of the original frame (and its contents) appears.

To move a frame, follow these steps:

1. Select the frame.
2. Click and hold on a relocator handle. Your pointer assumes the shape of a gripping hand.
3. Drag the frame to its new location and release the mouse button. Word Pro moves the frame to its new location and moves aside any text or objects currently there.

But I Wanted To Move the Frame on Top of Something Whether text wraps or doesn't wrap around a frame is controlled by settings in the Frame InfoBox. See "Aligning, Anchoring, and Wrapping Text around a Frame," later in this lesson, for help.

To delete a frame, follow these steps:

1. Select the frame to be deleted.
2. Press Delete.

Moving a Graphic within Its Frame

After you import a graphic, Word Pro places a standard sized frame around it. You can resize the frame to fit the graphic, or with the Frame InfoBox, you can ask Word Pro to resize the graphic to fit its frame. As a third option, you can move the graphic within the frame. If the graphic is too large for the frame, then part of the graphic is hidden or cropped; by moving the graphic within the frame, you can position the part you want to see within the frame window.

To move a graphic within a frame, follow these steps:

1. Double-click on the graphic to select it.
2. Click and hold the picture.
3. Drag the picture around within the frame. Again, if the graphic is larger than the frame, then only part of the graphic will be visible within the frame window.
4. Release the mouse button when the picture is where you want it.

Resizing a Frame

Both text and graphics frames are resizable by way of the resizing handles along their sides and corners. To resize a frame, follow these steps:

1. Select the frame to be resized.
2. Click on a resizing handle to grab it. To stretch a frame horizontally, grab a side handle. To stretch the frame vertically, grab a top or bottom handle. To stretch a frame along both axes at once, grab a corner handle.
3. Drag the frame to its new size. A shadow of the frame follows your pointer.
4. Release the mouse button. The frame is resized.

Aligning, Anchoring, and Wrapping Text around a Frame

Instead of moving a frame manually, you can align a frame against the margin or anchor a frame to a particular section of text. With an anchor, if the text moves on the page because of edits, the frame moves with it.

You can also control how text wraps around the frame. You can even force text (and other objects) to *not* wrap around a frame. This option allows you to place one graphic on top of another.

To align, anchor, or wrap text, use the Frame InfoBox. Follow these steps:

1. Right-click on the frame you want to change and select Frame Properties from the pop-up menu. Word Pro displays the **Frame InfoBox**, as shown in Figure 22.3.

Select how to align the frame.

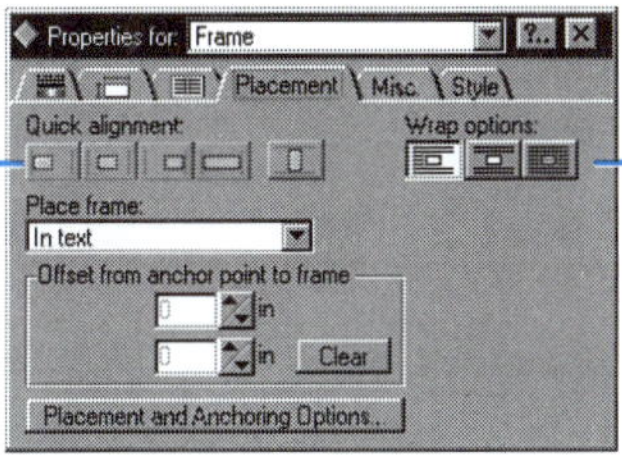

Select how you want text to wrap around the frame.

Figure 22.3 The Frame InfoBox.

2. Click on the Placement tab.

3. Under Quick alignment, you can align the frame relative to the margins by clicking on the appropriate button.

4. Under Wrap options, select how you want text (and other objects) to wrap around the frame.

5. To set an anchor, click on the Placement and Anchoring Options button. The Placement dialog box appears (see Figure 22.4).

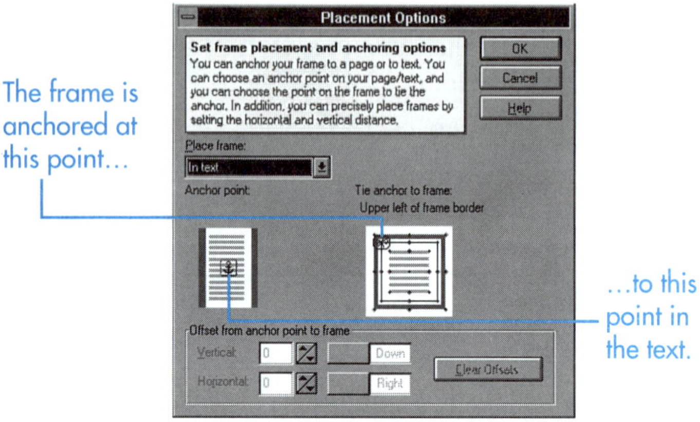

Figure 22.4 The Placement dialog box.

6. Select the component that the frame is anchored *to* from the Place frame list.

7. Select the part of the frame to which you want to anchor the text by clicking on that point in the diagram marked Tie anchor to frame.

8. Select the part of the text to which you want to anchor the frame by clicking on that point in the diagram marked Anchor point. For example, if you click on the upper right corner of the frame in step 7, and you click on the left edge of the text in step 8, then the right corner of the frame will be placed a certain distance from the left edge of the text.

9. To change the distance between the two points, enter vertical and horizontal distances in the boxes at the bottom of the dialog box.

10. When your frame is properly anchored, click on OK to close the Placement Options dialog box.

11. Close the Frame InfoBox.

> **My Frame Is Stuck!** If you try to move a frame and it won't budge, then it's probably because the frame is anchored. Simply remove the anchoring options to release the frame.

Adding a Background, Border, or Shadow to a Frame

You can change how a frame looks with the Frame Infobox. You can even "remove" a frame so that it doesn't print. Here's how:

1. Right-click on the frame and select Frame Properties. The Frame InfoBox is displayed.

2. Click on the Lines and Colors tab (see Figure 22.5).

3. Select a line or shadow option under Lines around frame.

4. If you want to, change the Line style, Line width, and/or Line color. Or you can select a custom frame style from the Designer borders list.

5. If you select the shadow option in step 3, select a different style under Shadow if you want to. Make additional selections under Shadow depth and/or Shadow color.

6. To control on which sides the border lines appear, make a selection under Line placement.

7. You can round off the corners with a selection under Corners.

8. To fill the frame with color, choose one from the Background color list. You can adjust the color fill by selecting a shading pattern from the Pattern list and a color for this pattern from the Pattern color list.

9. When you're done, close the Frame InfoBox.

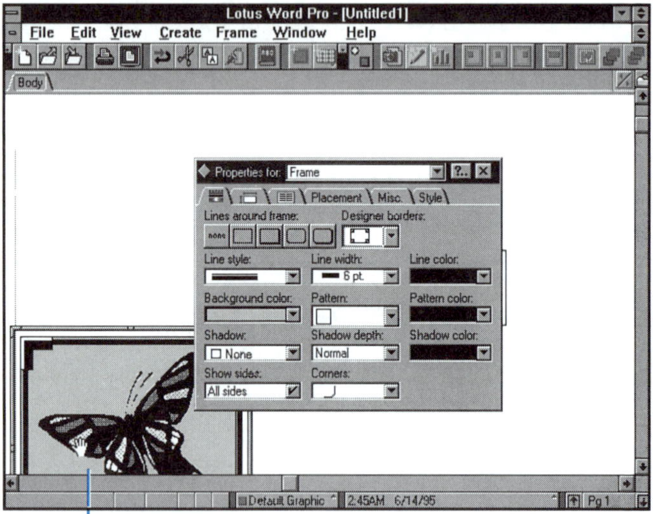

You can change the border style and fill color for your frame.

Figure 22.5 Change how your frame looks.

In this lesson, you learned how to copy, move, and delete frames. You also learned how to change a frame's properties.

Lesson 23

Using Text Columns

In this lesson, you'll learn how to create columns within your document for use in creating newsletters, information sheets, and reports.

Most columns are read down and then over, like a newspaper. These are called *newspaper columns*. A different type of column, *parallel columns*, are typically used to place headings across from paragraphs of text in another column. You might use parallel columns to create a sectioned header, or you might use them in a report. You'll learn how to create both newspaper style columns and parallel columns in this lesson. If you want to format information in columns that are read across, you will want to create a table. You'll learn how to create tables in Lesson 24.

Creating Newspaper Columns

Newspaper style columns are like the ones in newspapers; text goes down one column, then it flows over to the next column, and so on. You might use newspaper style columns in a company newsletter.

When you create columns, the change affects all the pages in your document. If you want to change only selected pages, you need to insert page layouts at key points. See Lesson 14 for help.

To create columns, follow these steps:

1. Right-click and select Page Properties from the pop-up menu. The Page layout InfoBox appears.

2. Click on the Columns tab (see Figure 23.1).

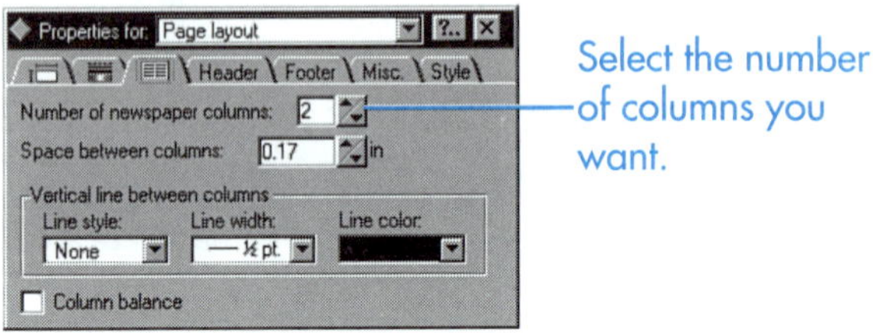

Figure 23.1 Creating newspaper columns.

3. Select the number of columns you want from the Number of newspaper columns box.
4. Adjust the width in the Space between columns box, if necessary.
5. To place a vertical separator line between columns, make your selections from the Line style, Line width, and Line color boxes.
6. To adjust the text in each column so that the bottom lines of text are even, select the Column balance check box.
7. Close the Text InfoBox.

Columns within Frames You can create newspaper columns within a text frame if you want to. Just create the frame and then use the Columns tab in the Frame InfoBox to insert columns. See Lesson 21 if you need help creating a frame.

Typing Text into Newspaper Columns

Typing text into columns is easy. Click once on the column to place the cursor there, and then type. When the text reaches the bottom of a column, the cursor shifts to the top of the next column, even if that column is on the next page. Here are some additional items to consider when working with columns:

- The bottom edges of the text in each column don't always appear even (especially on pages that are not full), unless you check the Column balance check box in the Page layout InfoBox.
- You may insert frames for text or graphics and make the text in each column flow around the frame.
- You may set text attributes, such as alignment, to give columns ragged or flush right edges.
- Each column is treated like a page, with its own margins you can adjust as necessary.

A *column break* stops the text flow in a column and picks it up again at the top of the next column. To insert a column break, follow these steps:

1. Place the insertion point where you want the column break to occur.
2. Open the Text menu and select Insert Other.
3. Select Column Break. Word Pro places a (nonprinting) break icon at the cursor, and then it pushes the text that follows the icon to the top of the next column.

Adjusting Newspaper Column Attributes

When you create columns in your document, they are of equal width. Often, in order to create visual interest, you may want to vary the size of your columns.

The margins for each column are shown on the Ruler, and they can be adjusted just like page margins. In addition, you can adjust the paragraph margins within each column. Figure 23.2

shows the column markings on the Ruler. To display the Ruler, click on the Show/Hide Ruler icon.

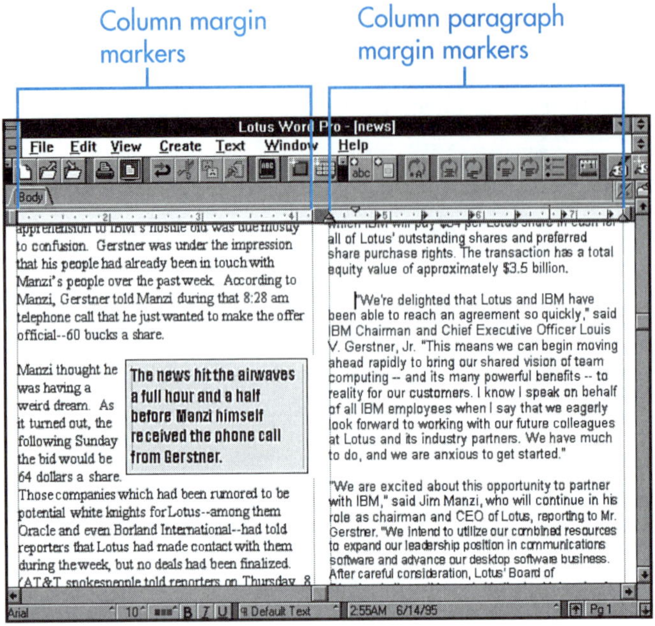

Figure 23.2 The margins for each column are shown on the Ruler.

To change the margin for a column, click on the column mark on the Ruler and drag it to the new location. Text is automatically adjusted to fit the new margins.

Creating Parallel Columns

Parallel columns combine the properties of newspaper columns and a table. Like newspaper columns, the contents in each parallel column are read down the page. But unlike newspaper columns, parallel columns can be placed on part of a page. In this way, parallel columns are like a table; they can be as big or as small vertically as you need. Figure 23.3 shows one use for parallel columns.

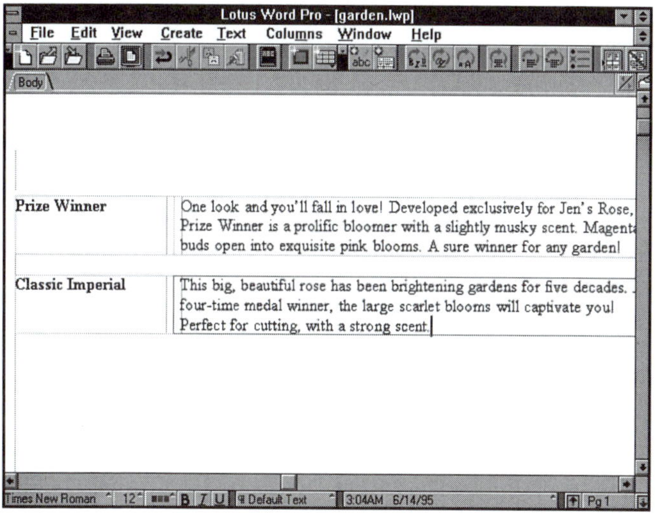

Figure 23.3 An example of parallel columns.

To create parallel columns, follow these steps:

1. Click on the Create Parallel Columns SmartIcon, or open the Create menu and select Create Parallel Columns. The Create Parallel Columns dialog box appears, as shown in Figure 23.4.

Create Parallel Columns icon

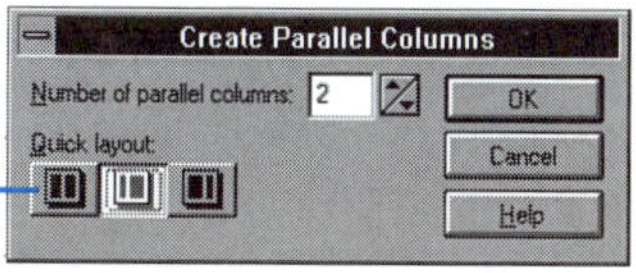

Figure 23.4 Where parallel columns are created.

2. Select the Number of parallel columns.

3. To make the leftmost or rightmost column in the set be less wide, click on one of the Quick layout buttons.

4. Click on OK. Word Pro creates parallel columns at the current cursor location. To type text into a parallel column, just click inside the column and type. Text wraps automatically within the column edges.

A parallel column has some of the attributes of a frame. Unlike a newspaper column, it's a box that is anchored to a point in text and can be dragged to a new location. Here are some tips for using parallel columns:

- To select a parallel column, click once on the column area. A column handle appears in the lower-right corner.
- To select the contents of the parallel column, click once on the column handle.
- To move a parallel column to a new location, first point to its border. The pointer will assume the shape of an open hand. Click and drag the column to the region of text where you want it to appear, then release the mouse button.
- To delete a parallel column, select its entire contents, then press Delete.

A parallel column has its own properties, which means that you can add borders, shading, background fills, and so on. None of these properties are new or exclusive to parallel columns; they've all been covered in prior lessons. Just right-click on the column and select Column Block Properties.

In this lesson, you learned how to create columns within your document. In the next lesson, you'll learn to create tables.

Lesson 24

Creating Tables

In this lesson, you'll learn how to build and manage tables.

Creating a Table

A properly formatted table presents data in an easily referenceable manner. Tables consist of rows (the *horizontal* axis) and columns (the *vertical* axis). A *cell* is formed where a row and a column meet.

You can create a table in Word Pro or import it from another source, such as Lotus 1-2-3. You can type text and even import graphics into a cell. You can format the contents of cells as well as the table itself. And if you need to make the table movable, you can place a table inside a frame.

To create a table, follow these steps:

1. Move the insertion point to the place where you want the table to appear. If you want to place a table inside a frame, then click inside the frame.
2. Click on the Create Table Grid SmartIcon. A grid appears, as shown in Figure 24.1.
3. Drag across the grid to select the number of columns and rows. Release the mouse button, and the table is created.

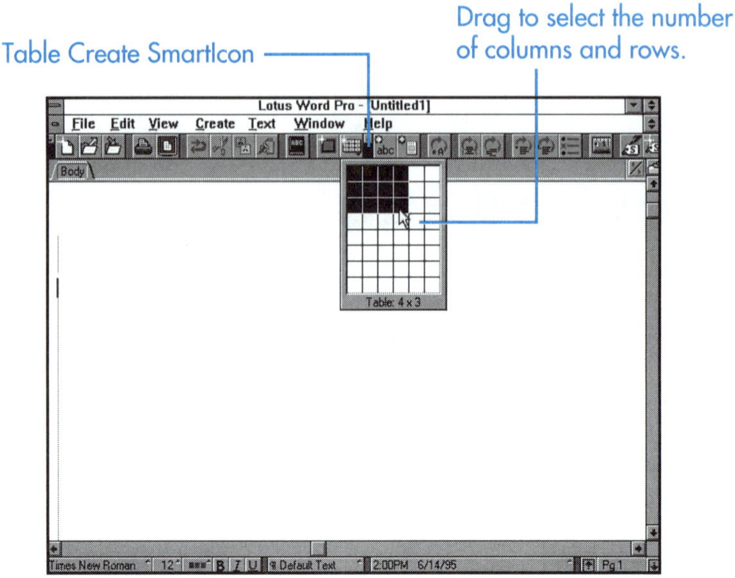

Figure 24.1 Creating a table.

Typing Information into a Table

You can type both numeric and text information into a table. You can also import a graphic into a cell.

To enter data into a table, follow these steps:

1. Click in a cell.
2. Type the data—text or numbers. You can format your numbers in various ways, as you'll see in a moment.
3. To move to the next cell, press Tab.

Totalling Numbers in a Column or a Row

Word Pro comes with the capability of totalling the values in a row or a column of cells. The total appears in another cell. To understand how formulas work, you have to understand how cells are identified or addressed. Each column in a table is assigned a letter, beginning with A. So the third column from the left is column C. Each row is numbered, beginning with 1. A cell's address is composed of its column letter and its cell number, so the second cell from the left in row 4 is cell B4.

Each formula begins with an equals sign. Use a plus sign (+) to indicate addition, a minus sign (–) to indicate subtraction, an asterisk (*) to indicate multiplication, and a slash (\) to indicate division. To total the two cells B3 and C3, you could type this into cell D3:

=B3+C3

I Can't Figure Out This Address Thing! Turn on the column and row markers by opening the View menu and selecting Set View Preferences. Click on the Show tab and select Show table row/col headings. Click on OK.

If you're going to total more than two cells, you might want to use the SUM function. With a function, you specify the range of cells you want to use, like this: B3..D3, which means cells B3, C3, and D3. So, to add a total to your table, just follow these steps:

1. Click in the cell in which you want the total to appear.
2. Open the Table menu and select Insert Formula. The Insert Formula dialog box appears.
3. Select the SUM function from the @Function list.
4. Click on Add to Formula. The function appears on the formula line (see Figure 24.2).

Replace the word "list" with the actual range to add.

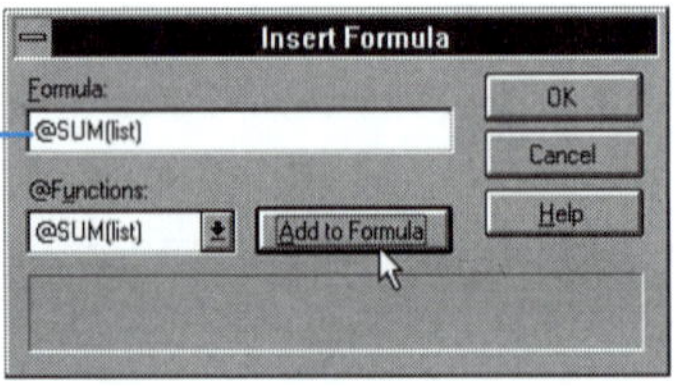

Figure 24.2 Totalling up.

5. Select the word list and replace it with the range of the cells you want to add, such as D2..D7.

6. Click on OK.

Wrong, Wrong If you get the formula wrong, just click in the cell, open the Table menu, and select Edit Formula to change it.

Copy That! You can copy a formula from one cell to another. For example, if you had a formula in cell D4 that totalled cells A4..C4, you could copy that formula to cell D5, and it would total cells A5..C5.

Editing Information in Tables

You can copy, move, and delete the contents of cells, but you must select them first:

- To select a cell, click on it. A cell handle appears in the lower-right corner. Click on the cell handle to select the contents of the cell.
- To select several adjacent cells, just click and drag over them.

- To delete the contents of a cell, select the cell, then press Delete. The cell remains at its present location; the table structure does not change.

Adding and Deleting Columns and Rows

To insert additional rows or columns, follow these steps:

1. Click within the table.
2. Click on the Insert row in table or the Insert column in table SmartIcon. A new row is inserted below where you clicked, or a new column is inserted to the right of where you clicked.

To delete a column or row, follow these steps:

1. Select the rows or columns you want to delete.
2. Click on the Delete selected columns in table or the Delete selected rows in table SmartIcon.

Formatting Cells

You can format text in cells just as you would format any other text. But to format numbers, you must use the Cell InfoBox. You can format numbers in various ways. For example, format a group of cells with the Currency format, and their contents appear with a dollar sign.

To change the format of a cell, follow these steps:

1. Select the cell you want to format.
2. Right-click and select Cell Properties from the menu that appears. If the cell is a formula cell, this option won't appear, so select Table Properties instead and then switch to the Table Cell InfoBox. The Cell InfoBox appears.

3. Click on the Number tab (see Figure 24.3).

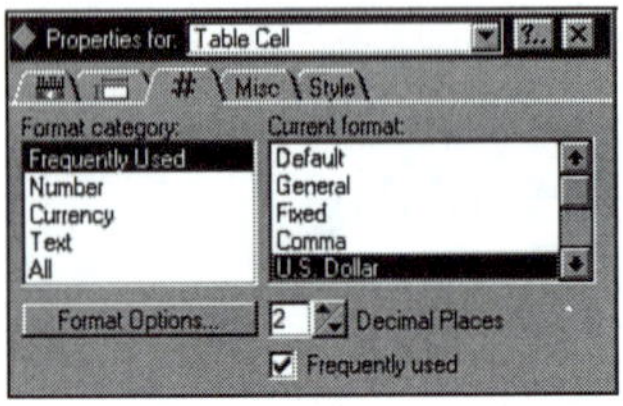

Figure 24.3 Use this InfoBox to format table numbers.

4. Select a Format category such as Currency.
5. Select a Current format such as U.S. Dollar.

Used a Lot If you see a format that you like in the Frequently Used category, you can simply select it and skip step 4.

6. Select the number of Decimal Places.
7. Close the Cell InfoBox.

You can also use the Cell InfoBox to add lines, shadows, and color to a cell (or group of cells).

The height of a cell adjusts automatically with its contents. So if you format text as 48 point, the cell gets taller to accommodate it. However, you must adjust the width of a column manually. Position the cursor at the right edge of a column. The cursor changes to a two-headed arrow. Click and drag the edge to adjust the size of the column.

Formatting a Table

Each table has its own set of properties, which you can change with the Table InfoBox. To access the InfoBox, right-click on a table and choose Table Properties from the menu that appears. Here you can select from these options:

- The first tab (the Lines and Color tab) allows you to choose a style for the table's outer border, as well as fill the table with color.
- The margins that surround the table may be set from the Size and Margins tab.
- The Placement tab lets you set anchoring options for the table. A table is anchored to a page or to a point of text in exactly the same way that a frame is anchored (frame anchoring was covered in Lesson 22).
- The flow of data between columns is controlled from the Misc. tab.
- The Style tab enables you to create named styles for well-formatted cells.

In this lesson, you learned how to create and edit tables. In the next lesson, you'll learn how a document can be reviewed and edited by more than one person.

Lesson 25

Working with a Team to Create a Final Document

In this lesson, you'll learn how use Word Pro in a team environment.

How the Team Concept Works

In a large organization, a document is often seen, reviewed, added to, cut from, and rewritten by a few dozen people. In Word Pro, a document can be made to keep track of its own revisions, who made them, and when. In addition, you can set up a document to provide only limited access to protect the original work from being edited by unauthorized personnel.

When an editor makes changes to a document, the edits show up in a designated color or style. Also, Word Pro keeps track of the *order* in which editors make changes to a document. For instance, one editor may make changes to the changes already made by a prior editor. Word Pro enables the author and editors to see a document in its various stages of development, the way it looked after it was passed from person to person to person. This way, either the author or an editor with authority can approve or disapprove all or only some of the changes made.

Setting Up the Team of Editors

To set up Word Pro to recognize multiple editors and make their changes visible in subsequent revisions, you invoke the TeamReview feature. Here's how:

1. Open the File menu and select TeamReview. The TeamReview Assistant dialog box appears, as shown in Figure 25.1.

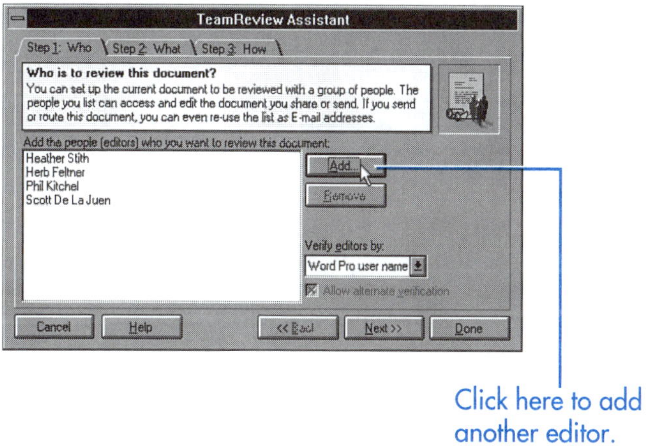

Figure 25.1 The first stage of TeamReview Assistant.

2. Click on the Add button. Type the name of the editor you want to add and click on OK. The new name appears in the list of valid editors. Note that this new editor must have access to a copy of Word Pro that is registered under this precise name.

3. After you add all your editors, click on the Next button to display Step 2 of the Assistant, as shown in Figure 25.2.

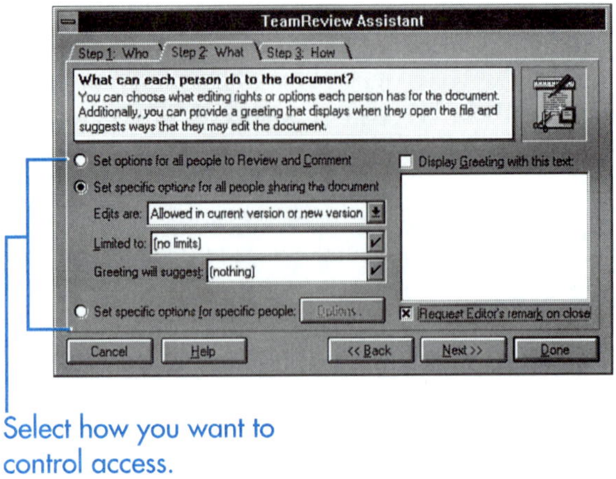

Figure 25.2 Deciding who gets to do what.

4. To restrict everyone to "comments" only, select Set options for all people to Review and Comment.

5. To restrict everyone to specific options such as making changes to the most current version of the document only or to saving changes and suggestions as a separate file, select Set specific options for all people sharing the document. Then make additional selections under the Edits are, Limited to, and Greeting will suggest boxes as needed.

6. To limit the types of edits specific editors are able to perform, click on Set specific options for specific people, then click on the Options button. Word Pro will bring up the Document Control dialog box, as shown in Figure 25.3.

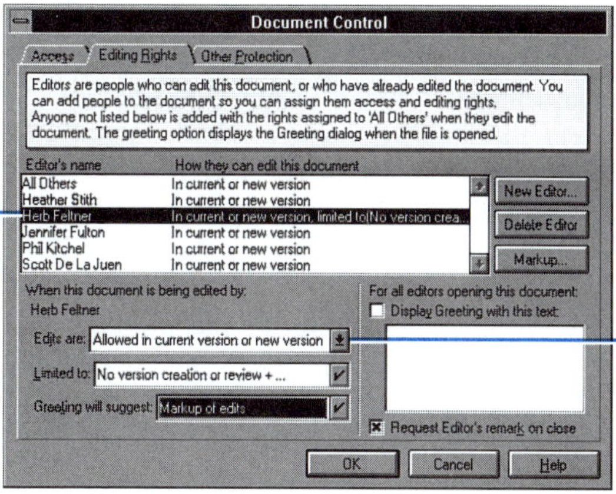

Figure 25.3 The Editing Rights page of Document Control.

7. To restrict rights for a specific editor, first choose that editor's name from the list, then set restrictions from the lists at the lower left. When restrictions are set, repeat for each editor, then click on OK.

8. To proceed to the next step in the Assistant, click on Next. The How page merely asks you how you intend to present this document to the editors you've listed. You may choose to send this document via e-mail or just distribute it on diskette. Word Pro can attach the document to the "outbox" of certain e-mail systems, as well as to distribution systems such as Lotus Notes.

9. To review your choices or to make any changes, click on <Back. Otherwise, click on Done.

10. If you chose to save the document revisions as a separate file, enter a filename and click on OK.

When New Editors Enter the Picture
To change the editorial review options for a document (or to add additional editors to the project), use the Document Control dialog box. Just open the File menu, select Document Properties, followed by Document Control.

Once everyone has a copy of the file, all they need to do is open the file and make changes. Later, when you consolidate all the different files, Word Pro will mark who changed what for you.

Consolidating the Edits

As part of the TeamReview process, several editors may each make individual changes or suggestions and save those changes as separate files. In order for you to decide which changes to accept and which to reject, it would be convenient if you could see all the changes all at once and compare them within the same window.

Word Pro allows you to do precisely that, through a process called TeamConsolidate. You use it to gather together all the separately revised files and view the changes to those files in one single document. (Of course, if everyone made their changes to one single document, you won't need to perform this function.)

To use TeamConsolidate, follow these steps:

1. Open the File menu and select TeamConsolidate. The TeamConsolidate dialog box appears.
2. Click on Add Files. Select a revised file and click on OK. The chosen file is added to the list of files to consolidate. Repeat for as many files as necessary.
3. To store the consolidation as a new version within this document, click on No, consolidate and markup into the current version of this document.

4. To place the consolidation into the currently open file, click on OK. Otherwise, click on Put the consolidated document into a copy of this file, then click on OK. The consolidation process will take a few minutes. Eventually, your document window will contain a consolidated form of the files you selected complete with markups, as in the example shown in Figure 25.4.

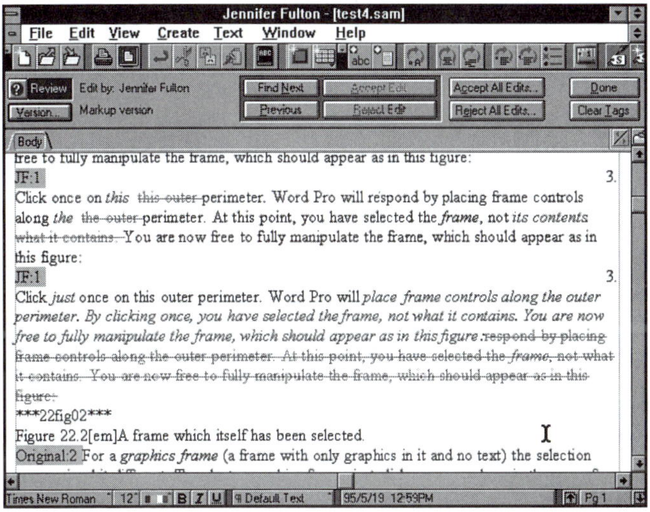

Figure 25.4 An example of a revised, consolidated document.

In a consolidated document, Word Pro goes to great pains to point out the differences between different editors' versions. Whenever a paragraph has been changed, Word Pro presents all the versions of the changed paragraphs, with the original placed first and the revisions next. Each changed paragraph is either marked at the beginning "Original" or with the name of its editor. The differences between the changed document and the original document are clearly marked. Additions are formatted in blue italic, with deletions in red strikethrough text.

Reviewing All Those Changes

After you consolidate your separate files, the Review bar appears at the top of the window. You use this bar to review all the changes that were made.

1. To find the first revision, click on Find Next.
   - To accept one of the editor's revisions, select the entire revision and click on Accept Edit.
   - To reject one of the editor's revisions and remove it from the current version, select the entire revision and click on Reject Edit.
   - You can accept or reject all the edits in one step by clicking on either Accept All Edits or Reject All Edits.
   - If you want to remove the remaining edit marks before you've reviewed the entire document, click on Clear Tags.
2. To close the Review bar, click on Done.

Creating Multiple Versions of the Same Document

Rather than keep multiple versions of the same document in separate files and consolidate them later, Word Pro gives you the option of maintaining all revisions to one document in a single file. With Version Control, you can review the changes you or anyone else made, "go back in time" to see how the document used to appear, and perhaps revert to the old form of the document if you deem it necessary.

One at a Time! The only negative to using Version Control is that only one person can work on the document at a time. If you need to work on the same document simultaneously, you should use the TeamReview approach discussed earlier.

Before an editor makes changes to a document, create a version for the editor:

1. Open the File menu and select Versions. The Versions dialog box appears for the current file, as shown in Figure 25.5.

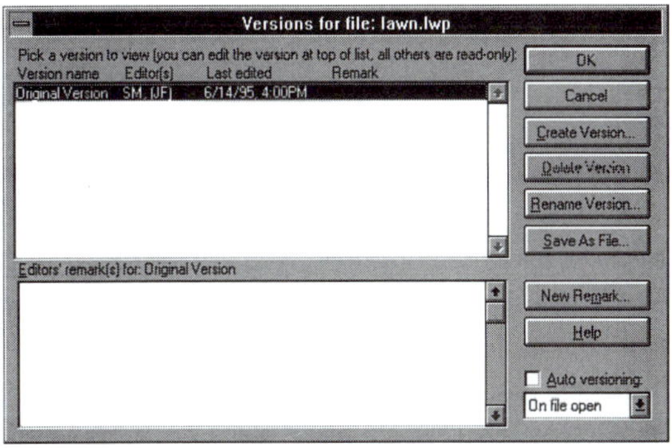

Figure 25.5 The Version control dialog box.

2. Every Word Pro file has at least one version, called the "Original Version." To begin a new version, first be sure the "original version" is the way you want it to appear whenever you review it. Then click on Create Version.

3. In the Create Document Version dialog box, enter a version name (*not* a filename) for the new version. Add a remark describing the reason for the revision under Editor's remark. Click on OK.

4. A message appears telling you that the new version has been created. Click on OK.

5. To begin editing the new revision, click on OK.

When you create a new revision, Word Pro enters your initials in the revision list and assumes that you're the editor of this revision. In order to place another editor's initials in this list, you have to *be* that editor. If you really have to, you could change the current user initials by opening the File menu, selecting User Setup, then selecting Word Pro Preferences. Click on the Personal tab, change the user information, and click on OK.

Marking Your Changes

Word Pro does not allow you to make changes to an old version of a document—only to the most recent version. Editors' revisions to the most recent revision will show up as markups, with the text attributes selected for each editor.

Before you begin making changes within your new version of the document, you might want to review and even change the text attributes assigned to you as an editor:

1. Open the File menu and select Document Properties.
2. Select Document Control. The Document Control dialog box appears.
3. Click on the Editing Rights tab.
4. Select an editor from the list and click on Markup.
5. Select the text attributes you want to assign this editor, then click on OK. Repeat steps 4 and 5 to change attributes for other editors.
6. Click on OK to close the Document Properties dialog box.

Now, once you have a version created and review how your changes will appear in the document, you're ready to make your edits. Follow these steps:

1. Open the Edit menu.

2. Select Markup Edits. Your changes will now be marked with the colors and text formatting assigned to you within the Document Properties dialog box.

Reviewing Changes

Once all the editors have made their changes, it's time to review them. Here's how:

1. Open the Edit menu and select Review Marked Edits. The Review bar appears at the top of the document window.

2. To choose a version to view, click on Version.

3. Select a version from the versions list, then click on OK.

4. To find the first revision, click on Find Next.

    - To accept one of the editor's revisions, select the entire revision and click on Accept Edit.

    - To reject one of the editor's revisions and remove it from the current version, select the entire revision and click on Reject Edit.

    - You can accept or reject all the edits in one step by clicking on either Accept All Edits or Reject All Edits.

    - If you want to remove the remaining edit marks before you've reviewed the entire document, click on Clear Tags.

5. To close the Review bar, click on Done.

In this lesson, you learned how to consolidate changes made to the same document by different editors. You also learned how to allow changes to one single document by several people. This is the final lesson. Good luck with Word Pro!

10 Index

A-B

C

D

E

F

G

H

I-J-K

T

U

V

W

X-Y-Z